T0013033

instruction to avoid common traps along your journey. I truly love the Coles, their lives and their ministry, and I'm thrilled for what they've given us. You'll want to read this book from front to back and over and over again. Not only that, make sure to get extra copies for friends and family, too."

Jennifer Eivaz, co-pastor, Harvest Church, Turlock, California; founder, Harvest Ministries International; author, *Prophetic Secrets* and *The Inner Healing and Deliverance Handbook*

"LaJun and Valora Cole are accurate prophetic voices being used by God in this hour. In *Divine Dispatch* they provide a blueprint to fulfill your prophetic destiny. This is a must-read for people who are serious about advancing in their God-ordained purpose! This book must be a tool in your prophetic arsenal."

Ryan LeStrange, senior leader, Ryan LeStrange Ministries

"I absolutely admire the ministry of Apostle LaJun Cole and Prophetess Valora Cole. They are truly apostolic leaders who have been sent to share divine insight and revelation for such a time as this. I believe this is the set time and season for *Divine Dispatch* to be released. The Coles bring clarity to the call, unlocking prophetic insight on the question so many people have: how to discover their assignment and how to develop into the person God ordained them to become. *Divine Dispatch* will bring awareness and understanding for many who are seeking answers regarding their purpose. Readers will receive impartation, revelation and activation. I highly recommend this book."

Sophia Ruffin, ambassador, Sophia Ruffin Global

"*Divine Dispatch* masterfully unlocks the code that will catapult you into your God-given destiny. You will receive insight and strategies that will change your life. The profound wisdom and astute understanding within every written word will help you navigate your pathway to the next level. *Divine Dispatch* is the guide for apostolic building and an instruction manual for the sent ones."

Andrew Towe, author, *The Triple Threat Anointing*; lead pastor, Ramp Church, Chattanooga, Tennessee

Divine
DISPATCH

Divine DISPATCH

DISCOVER, DEVELOP AND DEPLOY
YOUR KINGDOM ASSIGNMENT

LaJun Cole
and Valora Cole

Chosen
a division of Baker Publishing Group
Minneapolis, Minnesota

© 2022 by LaJun and Valora Cole

Published by Chosen Books
11400 Hampshire Avenue South
Minneapolis, Minnesota 55438
www.chosenbooks.com

Chosen Books is a division of
Baker Publishing Group, Grand Rapids, Michigan

Printed in the United States of America

Library of Congress Cataloging-in-Publication Data
Names: Cole, LaJun, author. | Cole, Valora, author.
Title: Divine dispatch : discover, develop and deploy your kingdom assignment / LaJun Cole and Valora Cole.
Description: Minneapolis, Minnesota : Chosen Books, a division of Baker Publishing Group, [2022] | Includes bibliographical references.
Identifiers: LCCN 2022014594 | ISBN 9780800762599 (trade paper) | ISBN 9780800762865 (casebound) | ISBN 9781493437634 (ebook)
Subjects: LCSH: Vocation—Christianity.
Classification: LCC BV4740 .C647 2022 | DDC 202—dc23/eng/20220505
LC record available at https://lccn.loc.gov/2022014594]

Cover design by Rob Williams, InsideOut Creative Arts, Inc.

Baker Publishing Group publications use paper produced from sustainable forestry practices and post-consumer waste whenever possible.

22   23   24   25   26   27   28   7   6   5   4   3   2   1

This concept was first given to us
when we were on a flight to Lima, Peru.
We never imagined that our shared Apple Note
would turn into this book.
Heavenly Father, thank You for entrusting us
with this revelation and the ability to birth it.

Contents

Foreword

I believe we are about to experience the greatest revival the earth has ever seen. This can only happen, however, as every believer is activated, trained and dispatched to take their place in the plan of God to advance the Gospel and expand the Kingdom. God is continually raising up new believers to advance the Kingdom of God and fulfill his purposes.

In their new book, *Divine Dispatch*, LaJun and Valora Cole give practical and biblical insight into the one question many believers are struggling to answer: *What exactly is my purpose and destiny in the earth, and why was I created?* When a person has clearly defined the answer to this one question, it can produce great increase in their life. I believe that every person who enters the world is designed and sent into the world with a distinct assignment by God.

Many who are currently reading this book are sent by God to fulfill an assignment in the earth. Many are sent to write books that educate believers; others are sent to provide clean water to citizens of nations where there is a lack of adequate drinking water. I also believe many are sent to prophesy, sent to preach, sent to pray, sent to heal, sent to deliver, sent to educate or even sent to restore hope to those who have lost hope.

I am always excited about new books released for the present generation. Over the last forty years in ministry, God has sent and divinely dispatched me to more than eighty different countries and an unknown number of regions and cities around the United States. I've written over forty books that have been sent to even more places than my feet have traveled to. I've had the honor of praying for, prophesying to, laying hands on and activating believers all over the world to fulfill their purpose and destiny. LaJun and Valora also have the vision to reach nations and activate believers. Their writings, including this book, are a part of fulfilling that mandate.

My prayer is that God would speak to you as you read the words of this book and stir in you the desire to learn more about your assignment in God's plan. Consider what they say, and may the Lord give you understanding.

One thing I've learned is that every person born has a desire to know they make a difference and their existence matters. But what most of us lack is the ability to define our purpose early enough in life, develop it and then commission it. This book will help every person expedite that process. LaJun and Valora clearly explain the process each believer must go through to navigate the challenges of discovering, developing and deploying their gift.

I personally know LaJun and Valora, and I know their heart is a heart of servitude and discipleship. I personally recommend this book and encourage individuals, leaders, ministries and churches to utilize it as a tool to assist believers to identify, master and dispatch their gifts.

May you be blessed and grow as you read it and gain the knowledge this book will impart.

Apostle John Eckhardt, overseer, Crusaders Church, Chicago, Illinois; bestselling author, *Prayers that Route Demons*

Acknowledgments

We want to say thank you to our spiritual parents, Dr. John and Wanda Eckhardt, for your spiritual impartation, unconditional love and continued support. You were dispatched by God to bless and have an impact on nations.

To our children, Kiara, LaJun Jr., Antoine, Diamond and David, and our grandchildren, Bailey, Braden, Aniyah, Major, David Jr. and LaJun III. We love you guys and appreciate you always standing behind us and believing in us.

A special thanks to our covenant sister, Jennifer Eivaz, for believing in us and standing with us through this journey.

Thank you to Dr. Shirene Anderson, a spiritual mother to the nations who stood with us from the concept to the completion of this book.

We appreciate our Contagious Church pastors, leaders, partners and our Contagious Connexion Fellowship. From the beginning, you have been a continued blessing. A special thanks to Reginald and Dr. Shanika Wingfield and Eliezer and Dr. Cindy Garcia for praying for and encouraging us every day of the project.

A big thank-you to LaJun and Valora Ministries partners and intercessors for your bountiful love and support.

Words cannot articulate how much we value and appreciate Kim Bangs and the Chosen Books family for believing in what God placed in our hearts to share with the world. Thanks, Lori Janke, for being an amazing copyeditor. Your excellence is amazing, and we look forward to experiencing what God has next for all of us.

Introduction

What Is a Divine Dispatch?

Not too long ago, Valora and I were traveling to Lima, Peru, at the request of a good friend who has a tremendous ministry there. I felt as if my assignment was very important, as is any assignment to deliver a message in the Kingdom of God. As we boarded the airplane, however, it began to dawn on me that what was bringing me to Peru was more than an invitation from a friend. I began to understand how important and serious my assignment was, and I felt immediately the burden to write about the call I was feeling. God had divinely implanted a message for me to carry to the members of my friend's church. This message was not mine, but a divine dispatch directly from Him.

During the flight, Valora and I began to write about what defines those who are sent: who God chooses, how they are called, how they discover their assignment, how they are developed and how they are deployed or used by God to advance His Kingdom on the earth. We wrote for the entire six-hour flight and completed six or seven pages of notes. We titled the project "Sent One."

In my military career, there were many times I was ordered from command to be sent on a mission. I was dispatched on missions and was expected to carry them out. Much the same, our heavenly Father chooses us and dispatches us with a message or a mission. The message we carry and the mission assigned to us are not our own. We have been entrusted with the message of another. We may be extremely passionate about it—in fact, we must be passionate about the message if we are to carry it and convey it well—but the message is not our own. It is the message of the One who sent us.

Many times, we do not realize the magnitude of the message or the messenger for whom we have been tasked to deliver. It is one thing to be asked by your friend to go to the store or to deliver a message to the bank. It is quite another thing for you to be asked by God to carry a message of the Gospel (the Good News) to someone.

This, my friend, is what we call a *divine dispatch*.[1] The word *divine* is defined as "relating to or coming from God or a god,"[2] and the word *dispatch* is defined as "to send quickly for a purpose."[3] We will start with John's account of the instructions Jesus gave the disciples. "Then said Jesus to them again, Peace be unto you: as my Father hath sent me, even so send I you" (John 20:21).

The word for *sent* that John uses in this context is the Greek word *apostello*, which means "to dispatch someone for the achievement of some objective."[4] The Greek word *apostello* is a combination of two Greek words: *apo* and *stello*. The prefix *apo* is a word that denotes "separation from a place or thing, something originating from or being sent away from."[5] The root word, *stello*, has a meaning of "preparing one's self, to set in order."[6] This word, *apostello*, can be understood in each of our lives. In essence, the sent one is divinely dispatched and given a message from God to a people group, a region or a nation.

When we look back over the course of our lives, we can see times and places for which we were being prepared. If we do not have the perspective that we are being prepared for a future assignment, we might wrestle with why we had to endure the various challenges and trials we experienced. We ask questions such as, Why did I have to go through that?

Valora and I have often asked God such questions. What we now know is that each part of our journey has taught us something different that made us ready to be sent or that helped us prepare for the assignment we are currently on. In fact, every part of our lives developed in us the message we are designed to carry.

Valora recalls a time in her life when God allowed her to experience a trial that prepared her to trust Him in spite of her circumstances. During her preteen years, her grandmother told her she was going to be used greatly by God to minister His Word. She was the first person to tell Valora this message. At sixteen, she was asked to speak at a youth conference. To her own surprise, she accepted.

It was an amazing experience for her, as she saw the demonstration of God's power while she ministered. After that, others asked her to minister, but she declined those invitations. Valora did not quite understand all that was happening in her life, and she began to shrink back because of fear. In her early twenties, she felt God call her. She asked God to show her His plans and confirm the call on her life, because she did not want to be disobedient to what God wanted her to do.

As she embarked on a three-day fast, she prayed that God would give her a sign regarding her purpose and destiny. That same week, she had a dream that she was in a field with the greenest grass she had ever seen. There were small white animals in the grass. As she started to go toward them to lay with them, a lady said they were not puppies but lambs. The woman continued and said Valora was to feed them.

She woke from that dream to a phone call from the lady who had been in her dream. She told Valora God was calling her into ministry, and she needed to obey. Later that day, she received another phone call from an older gentleman she admired. He told her she had been on his heart and that God had chosen her to minister His Word. He conveyed that she would reach many people and set them free. Yet another phone call came that afternoon from her pastor. As Valora began to speak with him about the dream and the other two phone calls, he encouraged her to surrender to God, accept the call and publicly acknowledge it during that evening's church service.

Valora felt she was too overwhelmed with the care of her sick child, the demands of her job and other personal situations she was dealing with to actively work in ministry. She knew ministry would bring added pressure. During the church service that evening, Valora acknowledged the call of God on her life and totally surrendered. She said that once she did, she felt free of the weight of fear she had been experiencing.

Not only was Valora free, but as she spoke out her willingness to minister, God demonstrated His power by healing and delivering members in the service. She continued to grow in her assignment as a minister. Even though there were times when the spirit of fear came to discourage her, she knew God was greater, and she continued to say yes to His will.

Another challenge Valora overcame was one she encountered a year and a half before we met. It was 2007, and she had been a nurse for over 24 years. She was serving faithfully in both her career and in the ministry when she became very sick. She initially ignored the symptoms and continued to push herself. When others asked if she was okay, she always replied she was fine.

She reached a point, however, when she could not keep up her busy pace. She had gotten very weak and had begun collapsing. When she found herself in crisis, she called a friend to let her know she was sick. This friend called an ambulance that came to take Valora to the hospital. She was admitted immediately, and after a series of tests, the doctors discovered her lungs were filled with fluid to the extent that her left lung was drowning. After further testing, the doctors discovered Valora had a brain tumor. This tumor was causing her body to shut down.

After a four-week hospital stay under the care of several specialists, she was told there was nothing else they could do for her. Their next step was to send her home and make her comfortable during what they saw as the last stage of her life. She was less than ninety pounds and was being given intravenous therapy of food, vitamins and minerals. At this point, Valora said to God that she was tired and ready to go to heaven. She thought, *If this is where my life ends, it is okay. I am ready.* She sensed the spirit of death in her hospital room. It was at this critical moment God spoke to her and said, *Valora, you cannot die, because your promise is still alive. You will live and not die and declare My Word.* She felt something shift within her, and the peace of God filled the room.

She was discharged with several medications to make her comfortable, but she was not able to take care of herself. She needed full-time assistance, so she moved into a friend's house to receive care. At the same time, God had given her a prescription. His orders were to take His Word three times a day and to partake daily in Communion. Two days after her discharge, she was sent back to the hospital due to difficulty with breathing and dehydration. She did not understand why this was happening to her. What she really wanted was to get back to her familiar way of doing life.

She said that even though this was the most challenging time in her life, she found the opposition she was experiencing was God's opportunity to use her to encourage and pray for the medical staff in the hospital. One evening, one of her doctors came to check on her. As he examined her, God began to speak words of encouragement to him through her. He began to weep and praise God for the answer he had prayed for.

One thing she did that caused her perspective to change was worship. When she chose to worship instead of worry, she saw her life and her future differently. It was during this time God told her she was going to get married and that her husband was on his way. He told her she and her spouse would do ministry together. She asked, *God, how can this happen with what is going on in my life right now?* In spite of her questions and doubts, God healed her completely without surgery, chemotherapy or radiation. Instead of taking the prescribed medications from her doctors, she believed God with a new level of faith. By the end of her healing, she received test results that revealed there was no longer a tumor. Her bloodwork was normal, and she was living on her own.

A year after her diagnoses, she visited the first church her parents had been members of. She had not been there in over thirty years. They had a guest speaker that day who was visiting from Memphis, Tennessee. She, the guest speaker and a group from the church went to eat together after the service. Two months later, she and the guest speaker were married. And yes, I was the guest speaker, and yes, God has used us together to do amazing things in ministry and business.

Valora now has the perspective that the brain tumor did not happen to her, it happened for her. It was the catalyst that brought her into a close relationship with God, and it prepared her to be the wife and pastor God chose her to be. This entire experience taught her not to look at her circumstances, but rather to trust God no matter what she sees. We can know for certain that God will never leave us or forsake us. God's Word and promise will always come to pass in our life. He will not allow anything to cause it to return void.

Jesus and Peter had a conversation in which Jesus told Peter that the devil wanted to sift him as wheat (see Luke 22:31–34). While Peter had no clue as to why the devil wanted to sift him, he did, at least, understand the terminology. Sifting was a process by which the good parts of wheat were separated from particles that were not good for use or consumption. Peter did not realize this process would be necessary for him to fulfill his destiny as a sent one. He would represent Christ on the earth after His return to heaven. Later, after many years had passed and Peter had grown older, he penned the words we find written in 1 Peter 5:10:

> But the God of all grace, who hath called us unto his eternal glory by Christ Jesus, after that ye have suffered a while, make you perfect, stablish, strengthen, settle you.

I love the wording of this text from the King James Version. Even though Peter had not understood Jesus' warning that he would be sifted, he learned in time that suffering makes us perfect. It establishes us, strengthens us and settles us.

There is a general process every sent one goes through prior to receiving his or her divine dispatch. First, there is a problem on the earth that needs a solution. Next, God dispatches a solutionist and develops within him or her the passion for the solution. Let's explore the process together as we look at four gospel passages.

Jesus told the disciples that even as He was sent (*apostello*), He would send them. The word Jesus used here is the Greek word *pempo*. This word means "to thrust a thing into another."[7] The disciples were being thrust into the same assignment He (Jesus) had been given. This assignment was to go throughout the world and make disciples who would turn the world upside down for the sake of the Kingdom.

Next, we will look at the instructions the gospel writer Matthew gave us concerning Jesus' final instructions to His sent ones.

> Go ye therefore, and teach all nations, baptizing them in the name of the Father, and of the Son, and of the Holy Ghost: Teaching them to observe all things whatsoever I have commanded you: and, lo, I am with you always, even unto the end of the world. Amen.
>
> Matthew 28:19–20

We have heard these words quoted many times, I am sure; however, few of us understand the depth of their meaning. John's gospel gives us a glimpse into the next steps of the early disciples of Christ, but Matthew's gospel gives us a much deeper understanding of what their assignment would be. Matthew uses the word *teach*, which in the Greek is *matheteuo*. This word means "to enroll as a scholar, to be a disciple of one or to make a disciple, or to teach or instruct."[8]

Matthew's interpretation of the assignment given to them by Jesus would resemble that of a young child entering kindergarten who is expected to complete a prepared curriculum that will lead him or her through his or her high school years, through post graduate work and matriculating with a doctorate degree. The assignment given to the early disciples was not simply that they were to go throughout the earth and make converts to Christianity. They were to teach, train, impart, activate and empower others to fulfill the commission of Christ.

They were to become ambassadors and partner with Him in completing His assignment on earth. Is it not wonderful to know that we, too, have been commissioned to be trained and prepared to fulfill the greatest assignment in the history of the earth? This assignment is to bring people to know God, Christ and the Holy Spirit in a more intimate way.

In the same sentence in which Matthew instructed them to teach, he also instructed them to baptize. The word *baptize* in the original language would have had a much deeper meaning than we might realize. It is the Greek word *baptizo*, which means "to make fully wet."[9]

Have you ever been exposed to rain or water to the extent that every part of you was immersed or made fully wet, fully soaked and completely submersed with water? This is the connotation of the text. In this case, instead of water, the substance is the character and nature of God, Christ and the Holy Spirit.

> Afterward he appeared unto the eleven as they sat at meat, and upbraided them with their unbelief and hardness of heart, because they believed not them which had seen him after he was risen. And he said unto them, Go ye into all the world, and preach the gospel to every creature. He that believeth and is baptized shall be saved; but he that believeth not shall be damned. And these signs shall follow them that believe; In my name shall they cast out devils; they shall speak with new tongues; they shall take up serpents; and if they drink any deadly thing, it shall not hurt them; they shall lay hands on the sick, and they shall recover.
>
> Mark 16:14–18

Notice that Mark tells them to preach, whereas Matthew told them to teach and baptize. It is interesting how each gospel writer further completes the thoughts of the others. Looking at each text allows us to gain a more complete picture of the assignment—the divine dispatch—they were given. Mark uses the word *preach*, which in the Greek language is *kerysso*. It means

- To be a herald, to officiate as a herald
- To proclaim after the manner of a herald
- Used with the suggestion of formality, gravity and an authority that must be listened to and obeyed
- To publish, proclaim openly something that has been done
- Used of the public proclamation of the gospel and matters pertaining to it, made by John the Baptist, by Jesus, by the apostles and other Christian teachers[10]

God dispatches them into the world and tells them, "Go ye into all the world and preach to every creature." He assures them that signs would follow those who believed. Is it not interesting that our modern-day Church has relegated the preaching and teaching of the Gospel to a certain few, such as pastors, evangelists and teachers? God's original intent, however, was for every believer to be responsible for spreading the Gospel and making it contagious. You may not be an ordained preacher, but you have a message, and you are sent with a word from Him. Look again at Mark 16 where He tells the disciples what they have the authority or power to do.

These signs shall follow those who believe:

- Cast out devils
- Speak with new tongues
- Take up serpents

- Drink anything deadly but it shall not hurt them
- Lay hands on the sick and they shall recover

Our final instructions come from the gospel writer Luke:

And he said unto them, These are the words which I spake unto you, while I was yet with you, that all things must be fulfilled, which were written in the law of Moses, and in the prophets, and in the psalms, concerning me. Then opened he their understanding, that they might understand the scriptures, and said unto them, Thus it is written, and thus it behooved Christ to suffer, and to rise from the dead the third day: And that repentance and remission of sins should be preached in his name among all nations, beginning at Jerusalem. And ye are witnesses of these things. And, behold, I send the promise of my Father upon you: but tarry ye in the city of Jerusalem, until ye be endued with power from on high.

Luke 24:44–49

Did you notice the last instruction? They were to wait until they were imbued with power from on high. If you remember in Luke 10, Jesus had already given them power. But the power Jesus is speaking of in this instance is a different kind of power. This power is from on high. This power came with demonstrations. It would produce evidence that they were who they said they were.

Here is a summary of the divine dispatch process:

1. There is a problem in the earth that needs a solution.
   - God births a solutionist for the problem.
   - The solutionist develops passion through life's processes. Note: Passion stems from something you love or hate.

2. God calls the sent one.

3. God sends someone to confirm His calling of the sent one.

4. God allows the sent one to go through a period of preparation, consecration and training.

   • God commissions the sent one.

   • God dispatches the sent one.

   • God gives him or her authority and power.

   • God backs up the sent one's message with signs, wonders and miracles.

As we come to understand the process, we find that all sent ones are divinely dispatched with a message, mission, mandate and mantle of Christ for His Church.

   • Message: core conversation and communication

   • Mission: assignment or instructions

   • Mandate: burden

   • Mantle: equipment

The first mention of Jesus dispatching the disciples was while He was still on the earth (see Luke 10:1–20). The text says Jesus dispatched them to every city to which He would eventually go. They were divinely dispatched as ambassadors to prepare the way for Him.

In verse nineteen, Jesus tells them He gave them power over all the power of the enemy. The word *power* used here by the gospel writer Luke is the Greek word *exousia*, which means "authority."[11] In essence, it is the delegated authority He gave them to carry out the assignment they would have on the earth; the assignment to continue the work He had been given from His Father in heaven.

In Acts 13, we find Paul and Barnabas being sent by the Holy Spirit to a group of cities that comprised Galatia, which is now modern-day Turkey.

> Now there were in the church that was at Antioch certain prophets and teachers; as Barnabas, and Simeon that was called Niger, and Lucius of Cyrene, and Manaen, which had been brought up with Herod the tetrarch, and Saul. As they ministered to the Lord, and fasted, the Holy Ghost said, Separate me Barnabas and Saul for the work whereunto I have called them. And when they had fasted and prayed, and laid their hands on them, they sent them away. So they, being sent forth by the Holy Ghost, departed unto Seleucia; and from thence they sailed to Cyprus. And when they were at Salamis, they preached the word of God in the synagogues of the Jews: and they had also John to their minister.
>
> Acts 13:1–5

As all sent ones who have been dispatched before you, you will find as a byproduct of your calling that you will encounter warfare. Because of this, it will be necessary for you to have the ability to

- Hear from God and speak only what He has spoken to you
- Know how to pray and intercede for yourself and others
- Know how to win souls who can join you in your assignment

Together, we will further unpack the process and give you tools we have learned to help us navigate it. Are you ready to join us as we discover, develop and deploy into our messages and missions as divinely dispatched by the King of kings? Let's get started!

STAGE 1

Discovery

There are diverse ways and times in which we discover our assignments. The word *discover* means "to get knowledge of, learn of, find or find out."[1]

There are many different means of discovery. Here are a few:

- Discovery in dreams
- Discovery by direct announcement from God
- Discovery by prophecy
- Discovery by prayer
- Discovery by angelic visitation

Some sent ones receive their calling or assignment at birth, while some find theirs in adulthood. Others have their calling revealed in dreams or by the prophetic declarations of parents, prophets or even God Himself. Yet others find their calling by angelic visitation. If you have not discovered your assignment via any of these methods, you will discover it over time. Life itself helps you identify what exactly is your calling and assignment. I have found that the definition of my calling has at times changed, migrated and matured. I have also watched as God has brought definition to the lives of many I mentor. We will talk about each of these pathways to helping us discover our divine assignments.

1

Discovery in Dreams

*O*ur first method of destiny discovery is through dreams. Joseph is a perfect example of one who discovered his individual destiny through dreams. He had an original dream, and then he had another to confirm his first (see Genesis 37). In his dream he saw himself in a place of authority as his siblings, father and mother bowed to him. As he got older, he found himself in a position of leadership in every situation in which he found himself.

Joseph's story begins when he was seventeen years old and was feeding his father's flocks alongside his brothers. The biblical narrative explains how Joseph had great favor with his father. His brothers noticed this favor and envied him because of it. Genesis 37 tells us, "And Joseph dreamed a dream, and he told it his brethren: and they hated him yet the more" (verse 5). He explained to them what he saw. In his dream, he and his brothers were binding sheaves in the field. Suddenly, his sheaf rose up and stood upright while their sheaves bowed to his (see verse 7).

While the Modern English Version translates this verse with the words "bowed to," the King James Version lends somewhat of a more detailed perspective. That version uses the word *obeisance*. The Hebrew meaning of the word *obeisance* is "to bow in token of respect or submission."[1] One could see why his brothers would be upset. The first question his brothers asked him was, "Do you think you will indeed reign over us?"

Not only would Joseph be a ruler over them, but he would be in a position that would cause them to have to bow in honor. This would have been quite a blow to their egos. First, Joseph was their father's favorite child. And second, Joseph was the child of Jacob's old age by Rachel, the wife he had desired from the beginning.

Jacob, who was Joseph's father, and his brother, Esau, were twins (see Genesis 25). They struggled in the womb, and as a result, Jacob came out holding his brother's heel. The story explains that Jacob's name meant supplanter, trickster and heel grabber. Jacob's mother received a prophetic dream that instructed her there were two nations in her womb and that the older would serve the younger.

The two boys grew, and Jacob's brother, Esau, became a very skilled hunter. As their father, Isaac, waned in strength and was near death, he told Esau he was hungry, and he asked Esau to go kill him some of the savory food he loved (see Genesis 27). He told him that once Esau brought him the food, he would bless him.

Jacob's mother, Rebekah, was listening, and she heard Isaac say he was going to eat the food Esau brought and then bless him before his death. Rebekah instructed Jacob to go to the flock and get two choice young goats. She assured him she would prepare them and make them savory as his father liked them. He did as she instructed.

Esau was a hairy man while Jacob's skin was smooth, and Jacob reminded his mother of this fact. He said that if his father discovered the deception, he would receive a curse. She assured Jacob that if there was any backlash from their scheme, it would fall on her. She then took the skin from the young goats and put it upon Jacob's arms and the back of his neck. His arms and the back of his neck would have been the places his father would touch if he reached out to embrace him. Placing a hand upon the back of the neck was a term of endearment from a father to a son.

When Jacob came to his father to bring the meal, something interesting happened. The Bible says Isaac's eyes were dim. Although it does not implicitly say his ears were hard of hearing, I believe this text gives us a clue about that. Jacob came to his father, and he called out to him. Isaac replied by asking the question, "Who are you, my son?" Jacob deceived his father and said he was his brother Esau, and he told his father he had brought him wild game to feed him. Isaac asked, "How is it that you have found it so quickly?" Although Isaac was old, his eyes dim and his ears hard of hearing, he knew it would have been difficult for Esau to have gone hunting and returned so quickly.

I remember going hunting with my grandfather when I was a young boy. We would have to either drive or walk to the hunting grounds. Many times, it was quite a while before we found the perfect location. Once there, we would set up and camouflage ourselves so that we could catch our unsuspecting prey by surprise.

I am not sure what technique Esau used to hunt, as the Bible does not clearly delineate, but one thing for certain is that Isaac knew it should have taken longer than it did to have gone hunting and returned with the food. Isaac still had discernment to know his touch would tell him which of his sons he was speaking with. He asked Jacob to come closer so that he could determine whether or not the son with whom he was speaking was really Esau. Jacob was prepared for this, as he knew Isaac would grab him by his hands.

He said, "The voice is the voice of Jacob, but the hands are the hands of Esau" (verse 22 MEV). He asked Jacob again if he really was Esau, to which Jacob replied yes. Isaac then ate the meal. After he was finished, he instructed Jacob to come near so he could kiss him. As Jacob drew closer, he smelled Esau's clothing that Jacob was wearing. Isaac then pronounced a blessing on Jacob, believing it was Esau.

> And he came near, and kissed him: and he smelled the smell of his raiment, and blessed him, and said, See, the smell of my son is as the smell of a field which the LORD hath blessed: Therefore God give thee of the dew of heaven, and the fatness of the earth, and plenty of corn and wine: Let people serve thee, and nations bow down to thee: be lord over thy brethren, and let thy mother's sons bow down to thee: cursed be every one that curseth thee, and blessed be he that blesseth thee.
>
> Genesis 27:27–29

Jacob left as soon as Isaac finished his prophetic declaration about his son's destiny. Shortly after, Esau walked in. When Isaac realized Jacob had tricked him, his heart was broken. At the same time, Esau was also heartbroken that his brother had tricked him—once again. He begged his father to find a word of blessing for him, and although it was not the blessing Jacob received, Isaac did bless Esau.

Jacob feared that his brother, Esau, would try to kill him, so he ran for his life to his uncle Laban. When Jacob arrived in the city where Laban lived, he ran into a young lady named Rachel who was at a well getting water for her flocks. Jacob fell in love with her, and he made an agreement with Laban that he would work seven years for him in exchange for his daughter's hand in marriage.

At the end of seven years when Jacob received his bride, he realized he had been tricked. He believed he had married the girl of his dreams, but he woke the next morning to find her tender-eyed sister, Leah, next to him instead. He then worked another seven years to wed her sister, Rachel, whom he had desired from the beginning. On top of that, he worked another six years for his uncle. I have always wondered whether or not Jacob would have experienced this deceit if he had not tricked his brother out of his birthright and blessing.

During his years working for his two wives, he produced thirteen children by four women. His children by Leah were Reuben, Simeon, Levi, Judah, Issachar and Zebulun, and by her concubine, Zilpah, he produced Gad and Asher. His children by Rachel's servant were Dan and Naphtali, and his children by the wife of his dreams were Joseph and Benjamin. Joseph was Jacob's eleventh child, and his brothers both envied and were jealous of him.

The Bible tells us Joseph had a coat of many colors. His father had neither sewn nor dyed a coat with multiple colors for any of his other sons, so I am sure this added to their jealousy. Imagine that your father had eleven children, but for only one did he go out of his way to have a special coat created that signified his unique and special love. I have no idea what it would have cost to create such a coat, but make no mistake about it, that was a very special gesture. It made him stand out from his siblings.

Genesis 37 tells us Joseph had yet another dream (see verse 9). One thing we have learned in studying the Bible is that when you have back-to-back dreams, God is about to do something. The second dream confirmed the fact that, not only was the first dream from God, but what He revealed in the first dream would come to pass. Joseph shared his second dream with his brothers. He told them that the sun, moon and eleven stars were bowing to him.

His brothers were already envious of him, but I am sure this second dream made his brothers even madder. When he told his father this dream, his father rebuked him and asked, "Shall I and thy mother and thy brethren indeed come to bow down ourselves to thee to the earth?" (verse 10). The Bible tells us his brothers became even more jealous, but his father, "observed the saying" (verse 11).

I find it interesting that the Bible notes that Jacob observed the dream. The word *observed* used in this sentence means "to watch and wait for."[2] In essence, Jacob had enough experience with God to know God could do whatever He wanted to do. He knew that as God had preserved his life and rescued him from dangers far and near, He would bring to pass this word for Joseph's future. He remembered how his father had prophesied accurately about what his destiny and calling would be. Having had that history with God, he knew this dream about Joseph's life and purpose would also come to pass.

You also must remember that nothing can stop God's plan for your life. Joseph's brothers attempted to assassinate him, but God had the assassination attempt stopped (see Genesis 37:20–28). He was delivered to Potiphar's house where he found grace in Potiphar's sight, and he was promoted to a position of leadership; however, Potiphar's wife lied about something she claimed Joseph had done, and the result was that he was imprisoned (see Genesis 39:7–20). No matter what happened, each situation placed him closer to his destiny.

While in prison, it appeared that God's plan for him was not going to come to pass. But make no mistake about it—Joseph was sent by God. He was placed strategically by God every step of his journey to put him in position to solve the problem of food shortages in Egypt. While still in prison, two prisoners came to Joseph to inquire of him concerning their dreams (see Genesis 40:5–23). He interpreted their dreams, one of whom was promoted while the other was executed.

The butler was promoted to chief butler and was restored to the king's court. It probably seemed to Joseph that he had been forgotten; however, when God has a plan, nothing can stop it from coming to pass. Pharaoh had a dream that could not be interpreted (see Genesis 41). The chief butler remembered Joseph and told Pharaoh about Joseph's ability to interpret dreams. Joseph was called from prison to stand before Pharaoh, and he interpreted Pharaoh's dream correctly.

Because of his wisdom and discernment, Joseph was put in a position of leadership to help Egypt through the coming seven-year famine. God gave him the strategy of saving food during the seven years preceding the famine so that there would be a surplus of food during the seven years of lack.

As we see in Joseph's life, God can help us discover our assignment through dreams. Joseph was a sent one who was divinely dispatched to rule and reign in Egypt and to save Egypt from starvation. Eventually, he saw his brothers and his father again.

I remember God speaking to me in a dream about a part of my destiny. In this dream I saw myself preaching. I was in a white robe preaching with power and fire and ministering in a church. When I finished preaching, I saw myself laying hands on and praying for different people in the audience. As I prayed with each of them, they were slain in the Spirit. I asked a spiritual father what this dream meant, and he shared that the white robe symbolized purity. It also represented much of what my ministry would be about.

I have found that much of my personal ministry revolves around discipling believers and being pure before the Lord.

And usually, my preaching is with fire. I often teach, but when the Spirit of the Lord stirs in my heart, I preach with fire. God gave me a small glimpse of what I would be doing, but He did not show me what my process would be like to acquire the fire. He often does not show us specific details, because if He did, most of us would run. I sure would have. I will share more on my personal process of development in the next section.

QUESTIONS TO
Ponder

1. Has God ever spoken to you in your dreams about your purpose and assignment?
2. Do you dream frequently?
3. Have you ever seen yourself ministering or speaking to others in your dreams?
4. What were you wearing (such as colors)?
5. What was your message?
6. Who were the people you were speaking to?

Prayer

to Activate Your Dream Realm and Asking God to Speak to You Through Your Dreams

DEAR HEAVENLY FATHER, *I come to You knowing You are the Almighty One who hears me when I pray, and You are the*

God who answers. I stand on Your Word from Joel 2:28 that says that in the last days You will pour out Your Spirit upon all flesh. Your sons and daughters will prophesy, old men will have dreams and young men will see visions. As one of Your children, my heart's desire is to be able to dream of only what You have released. I ask to be able to understand dreams and visions of various kinds. Lord, activate my dream realm that has been dormant, and help me to see into the night. I call for good and inspiring dreams and visions to come to pass.

Lord, speak to me in my dreams. Reveal Your heart, open my eyes to see my purpose and destiny and expose every plot of Satan against my life and others. Open my eyes to see images and scenes clearly, open my ears to hear sounds and voices distinctly and open my heart to perceive and understand what You are saying in my dreams. I pray for accurate interpretation of dreams and visions in my life and in the lives of others.

I plead the blood of Jesus over my life, and I cover my sleep stages against interruption. I ask that You prevent my dreams from being infiltrated and disturbed by demonic forces. I call forth and release any dream or vision that has been held up. I cancel every spirit of nightmares and bad dreams from attacking me while I sleep. I cast all nightmares and bad dreams upon You and forbid them from manifesting in my life. My dreams will not be disrupted, hindered or stolen. I will remember my dreams and recall those I have forgotten.

I apply the blood of Jesus over my dreams. I will not be anxious; I will not toss and turn nor be afraid during the night when I sleep. When I lie down, my sleep will be sweet. Upon awakening, I will be refreshed, renewed, revived and restored with enough rest and energy to accomplish the tasks You have given to me for the day. In Jesus' name, Amen.

2

Discovery by Direct Announcement of God

*S*aul of Tarsus was walking down the road to Damascus, Syria when a light shined around him (see Acts 9). A voice called from heaven and asked Saul how long he would "kick against the pricks" (verse 5). Farmers placed pricks, which were boards with nails or spikes on them, behind the oxen's legs to keep them headed in the right direction. If an animal did not want to go forward, its leg would bump into the prick. This caused the animal to continue in a forward direction.

Saul asked the question, "What wilt thou have me to do?" (verse 6). The Lord then instructed him to rise up and go into the city. He assured Saul that when he arrived there, he would be told what he is to do next. The text goes on to say that for three days Saul was without sight.

At the same time, the Lord spoke through a vision to a disciple in Damascus named Ananias. He instructed Ananias to go to Straight Street and inquire of a man named Saul of Tarsus. He was told Saul would be expecting him because he also had received a vision. In Saul's vision, he saw a man named Ananias putting hands on him so that he could receive his sight back.

Ananias was concerned and somewhat afraid. He reminded God that this same Saul had letters from the chief priests to bind all who called on His name. God shared with Ananias that Saul would be divinely dispatched by Him to bear His name before the Gentiles, their kings and the sons of Israel. The Bible tells us that once Ananias laid his hands on Saul, the scales fell from his eyes, and he ate and was strengthened (see Acts 9:9–18).

Paul received more than natural sight that day. The Bible tells us he was also filled with the Holy Spirit. He stayed in Damascus for several more days with the disciples and began to preach that Jesus was the Son of God. Paul continued to do exactly the things God had told Ananias he would; he preached to the Gentiles, to their kings and to the sons of Israel.

QUESTIONS TO
Ponder

1. Have you ever heard God speak directly to you about your calling?

2. Is it possible God was speaking but you were not listening?

3. Is it possible God was speaking but you ignored Him?

4. What can you do to position yourself to receive more communication from God?

Prayer

for God to Speak Directly to You
and to Clarify Your Assignment

FATHER, *in Jesus' name, I praise and worship You as the Most High God. I come to You because You are my Creator who established my destiny before the world began. Because Your ways and thoughts are higher than mine, I do not always know what is best for me. In times of uncertainty, I need Your guidance.*

You are Jehovah Rohi, my Shepherd, the One who leads and guides me in the way I should go. I surrender myself to be led in the paths of righteousness that I may fulfill Your perfect will. You are my Jehovah Shalom, the peace that goes beyond my understanding, when I am unsure of what I am called to do. With so many voices I hear, including my own, I need clarity on what You have called me to do—not what I want to do or what others think I should do. In the past, I have listened to the wrong voices and have at times gotten sidetracked from my assignment.

Please forgive me for when I procrastinated or rebelled against Your instruction. I exchange my will for Your perfect will. I take authority over false assignments and silence every voice of my past, every voice that is connected to fear and every voice that is contrary to Your will for my life. Father, I declare that I hear Your small, still voice, and I will not follow any other voice.

I know the call on my life is great. Help me to discern between a great idea and a God-idea. I cannot afford to operate under what appears to be something good. I must seek after the God-ideas that are connected to my purpose, which is to bring healing, restoration and deliverance to others. Being in Your perfect will always brings me the best results, and I will be rewarded for my obedience. Father, above everything else, I want to please You. Let Your will be done in me, even as it is in heaven. In Jesus' name, Amen.

3

Discovery by Prophecy

nother way to discover your calling is by prophecy. As I referred to earlier, in Luke 22, Jesus had a discussion with Peter. I am almost certain Peter did not like the conversation, but it was necessary. Jesus began by calling Peter by his surname, Simon. He released a prophetic word to him about his future assignment for the Kingdom.

> "Simon, Simon, listen! Satan has demanded to have you to sift you as wheat. But I have prayed for you that your faith may not fail. And when you have repented, strengthen your brothers." He said to Him, "Lord, I am ready to go with You to prison and to death." He said, "I tell you, Peter, before the rooster crows today, you will deny three times that you know Me."
>
> Luke 22:31–34 MEV

Fortunately for Peter, that was the end of that conversation. But it was not the end of the story. I am not sure how Peter must have felt. He had just been told what his assignment was going to be; however, in the same sentence and breath, he was also told he would deny his master—not once, but three times. Luke is the only gospel writer to share the story of Peter denying Jesus. As Luke's testimony was not a first-hand account of the story, he had to have received his version from Peter. Ironically, Peter asked him to include the story of his denial. Luke also mentions Peter's reaction to Jesus' observance of Peter's denial.

And when they had kindled a fire in the midst of the hall, and were set down together, Peter sat down among them. But a certain maid beheld him as he sat by the fire, and earnestly looked upon him, and said, This man was also with him. And he denied him, saying, Woman, I know him not. And after a little while another saw him, and said, Thou art also of them. And Peter said, Man, I am not. And about the space of one hour after another confidently affirmed, saying, Of a truth this fellow also was with him: for he is a Galilaean. And Peter said, Man, I know not what thou sayest. And immediately, while he yet spake, the cock crew. And the Lord turned, and looked upon Peter. And Peter remembered the word of the Lord, how he had said unto him, Before the cock crow, thou shalt deny me thrice. And Peter went out, and wept bitterly.

Luke 22:55–62

I am sure there have been times we have been Peter in this story. The passage says Jesus looked at Peter as he denied Him, and Peter remembered the words He had spoken earlier.

Someone who was serving beside me once said to me, "I'm with you. I got nowhere else to go." The line comes from the movie *An Officer and a Gentleman*. Richard Gere plays a Navy Aviation Academy student named Zack Mayo. He says to his training officer, named Sergeant Emil Foley and played by Louis

Gossett Jr., "I got nowhere else to go."[1] The scene happens when Louis Gossett, who is Richard Gere's drill instructor at his flight school, is giving Richard Gere a good old-fashioned drill sergeant smoking. Eventually, Louis Gossett tells him he was out (which means he was kicked out of the school). In tears, Richard Gere says, "Don't you do it! Don't you say it! I got nowhere else to go."

Unfortunately, like Peter who told Jesus initially that he would be with Him no matter where He went, this young man eventually found somewhere else to go. Peter had said he was ready for prison and death, and yet he denied Him. Luke records that after the denial happened, Peter went out and wept bitterly.

Jesus also foretold that Peter would go and strengthen his brothers after he had been converted (see verse 32). Every prophetic word Jesus spoke to Peter came to fruition. Yes, Peter denied Jesus, but God also used Peter mightily. On the day of Pentecost, he stood up in the middle of the disciples and preached to them—just as Jesus said he would.

QUESTIONS TO
Ponder

1. Are you open to receiving prophecy?
2. Have you received a word of prophecy about your destiny?
3. Have you written down the different prophetic words?
4. Remember that God does not always speak directly through a person. He sometimes prophesies through a person's circumstances and situations.

Prayer

for God to Open Your Mind to
Receive the Prophetic Word

JEHOVAH, *I adore and worship You as the Most High God.
You are the author and finisher of my faith. I am confident
that what You started in me You will complete. There have been
times I have questioned whether or not I could be used by You,
or whether or not I was qualified to do what You have asked
me to do. Today, I present my body as a living sacrifice to be
transformed by the renewing of my mind to see myself the way
You see me. Thank You for the thoughts You think toward me;
thoughts of peace and not of evil, to give me hope and a future.*

*God, I know You use prophetic voices throughout the earth to
speak Your heart into the lives of others. Father, give me insight
and discernment as to who communicates Your prophetic voice
that I may receive from them. Help me to recognize those who
are false prophets so that I may reject those voices.*

*Search my heart for any areas that have been closed to
receiving Your word, whether through unbelief or fear. Open
my heart and mind to accept the word You have sent to build
my faith. Help me to listen to the word You have sent to com-
municate what You are doing now and what will be revealed
in the time to come concerning me and those around me. Let
every false prophet be exposed and removed from any sphere
of influence. I will reject and cast down every false prophetic
word given to me.*

*Lord, I give You the right to remove anything that has hin-
dered, blocked or prevented me from receiving what You are
saying through Your prophetic voices concerning me and the
call You have on my life. Open my eyes and my understanding*

to receive the instruction and revelation knowledge You are speaking to me. Your word is prophetic; it brings clarity, it foretells what is to come, it brings instruction of the things I need to do and it builds me up.

I receive Your word to guide me in the way I should go and to give me clarity in what is required of me. Let the prophetic word confirm what You spoke in my spirit. Help me to stand on it and not waver or be double minded. I wage a good warfare for every prophetic promise concerning me, and I hold on to it without wavering. Even if heaven and earth pass away, Your word will always remain. Thank You, Father, for watching over Your Word and making sure it is fulfilled and manifested in my life. In Jesus' name, Amen.

4

Discovery by Prayer

ssignments of sent ones can be discovered through prayer. In the book of Acts, the prophets and teachers in Antioch, namely Barnabas, Simeon, Lucius of Cyrene, Manaen and Saul (Paul) were in prayer (see Acts 13). As they worshiped and fasted, the Holy Ghost said, "Separate me Barnabas and Saul for the work whereunto I have called them" (Acts 13:2). After fasting and praying, they laid hands on them and dispatched them. I am sure no one could have told Paul and Barnabas all they would encounter when they departed on their first missionary journey.

If you have ever heard us minister at our local church in Tampa, then you know we have memorized Paul's missionary journeys. He leaves Antioch of Syria and goes to the Island of Cypress. There they, Paul and Barnabas, pass through the island. They start at the northern end and journey to the south-ernmost tip. They depart from Cypress and journey by boat to modern-day Turkey, journeying through Antioch of Psidia, Iconium, Derbe and Lystra. This is his first missionary journey.

My prayer is that we really dive into this story and learn all Paul had to endure on his first missionary journey. Many times, believers do not count the cost of what the early disciples and apostles encountered as they accepted the call of God on their lives. We need to know the miles they walked, the tears they cried and the bruises they received along the way. Through it all, God was with them.

I pray that we receive the courage to walk out what God asks us to do despite the odds, adversity and obstacles we face. For Paul, this clearly was not an easy journey as he strove to complete his assignment; however, he was fully persuaded and committed, and God was faithful.

QUESTIONS TO
Ponder

1. How often do you pray about purpose, destiny or assignments?
2. Do you pray and wait for God to speak?
3. Keep a journal to write down any prophetic words God speaks to you during worship and prayer.

Prayer

for God to Speak to You About
Your Purpose Through Prayer

ABBA, FATHER, *thank You for Your continued, unconditional love for me. Thank You for loving me so much that You sent Jesus to die for me so that I could be redeemed and have an abundant life. I repent of any wrongdoing and the times I have fallen short of Your glory. Thank You for the power of the blood of Jesus that allows me the opportunity to come boldly before Your throne to obtain mercy and find grace and help in a time of need.*

I seek You with all my heart, mind, body and soul so that I may know the full purpose of why I was born, why You chose me and why You sent me into the earth. I have had many plans for my life, but I know it is Your purpose that will ultimately prevail. I trust in Your thoughts and plans for me; therefore, I come into alignment with them and do not rely on my own understanding of what I should do. In all my ways I desire to acknowledge You so that You will order my steps in the right path.

Lord, I seek You first for clarity about my purpose for this season so that I do not operate from the purpose of an old season. I pray for fresh vision to see plainly as You see and ears to hear what You are saying for my life. Even when things around me do not look, feel or sound good, Your Word promises You will make sure it all works together for my good, because I love You and I am called according to Your purpose. I realize that even trials, my pain and the disappointments of life serve a purpose.

I ask in faith for daily wisdom for every decision I need to make in fulfilling my purpose. Because You are my present help, I receive Your daily provision. Today, I walk in new revelation, clarity, knowledge and understanding with confidence and boldness without wavering, procrastinating or second-guessing what You have for me to do. Because You are Alpha and Omega, You are faithful to complete in me what You started. In the mighty name of Jesus, Amen.

5

Discovery by Angelic Visitation

God can dispatch angels to give us direction concerning our purpose and destiny. I have had several angelic visitations in my life. I remember each encounter as if it were yesterday.

One of my first encounters was when God sent an angel to rescue me as I was stranded on the side of the road in Louisiana. It was 1992, and I was stationed in the army at Fort Polk, Louisiana. I was driving home to Arkansas for Thanksgiving in my brand new 1972 Ford Thunderbird. It may not have been new to anyone else, but to me it was brand new. Suddenly, the engine began to sputter, and the car eventually cut off.

I found myself on the side of a long, dark and isolated road. I was driving with my son, LaJun Jr., who was about three years old. He was in the back seat crying something fierce, so I began to pray. *Lord, send help.*

Moments after I began to pray for the Lord to send help, a van pulled up behind me. A gentleman walked up behind the car and around to the driver's side. He said that God had sent him to get us. I asked him several times that night how he really got there, but each time he stated that God had sent him. In other words, God had divinely dispatched him to come and help us. He put us in his van and drove us back to a hotel. He even paid for the hotel.

I believe this was, in fact, an angelic encounter. I believe God releases and sends angels to speak to us. I will never forget that night. I believe with everything within me that I encountered an angel. The Bible says, "Be not forgetful to entertain strangers: for thereby some have entertained angels unawares" (Hebrews 13:2).

Zachariah, Elizabeth, Joseph and Mary also encountered angels. Do you remember the stories of how Mary and Elizabeth discovered their divine mandates and the divine mandates of their sons?

The Angel of the Lord Visits Zechariah and Elizabeth

The book of Luke in the Bible tells the story of Zechariah, who was a priest serving in the temple (see Luke 1:5–22). The biblical writer narrates the story of Zechariah, telling us he was well advanced in years, he had no children and his wife was barren. As he was serving his priestly duty in the temple, an angel of the Lord who was standing beside the altar of incense appeared to him. Initially, Zechariah was troubled and fearful, but the angel assured him he meant him no harm.

He tells Zechariah his prayer has been heard and his wife will bear a child. He goes on to tell him the child will be great in the sight of the Lord, and from his birth he will be a Nazarite who is filled with the Holy Spirit. The angel also tells Zechariah what his son's divine assignment will be. He shares that John's assignment will be to make ready a people who are prepared for the Lord. He was to turn the sons of Israel back to love their God and to turn the hearts of the fathers to the children.

Unfortunately, Zechariah then asks a question that got him into trouble. He asks how this could happen. He then explains to the angel that he and his wife are old. Gabriel reminds him that he is an angel of the Lord, that he stands in the presence of the Lord and that he was sent (divinely dispatched) from God. He then tells Zechariah that because he did not believe the words he was speaking, from that moment until the birth of his child he would be silent and unable to speak. When he came out of the temple, he could not speak. He made signs to the people but remained speechless.

The Angel of the Lord Visits Joseph in a Dream

The book of Matthew chronicles Jesus' birth. In this telling of His birth story, we see the angel of the Lord having a conversation with Joseph concerning marrying Mary (see Matthew 1:18–24). He shared that Mary, the woman to whom he was engaged, was pregnant with a child from the Holy Spirit.

I am not sure how other people would have handled this, but Joseph handles it as well as could be expected. I am sure there must have been some concern about marrying her in this condition as well as raising the child. In this scenario, the angel tells Joseph not to fear taking Mary as his wife. He goes on to give instructions concerning Jesus' destiny. He tells Joseph, "He shall save his people from their sins" (verse 21).

The gospel of Matthew is a letter written to us from the perspective of Jesus as King. The earthly lineage, which the writer gives us in verses 1–17, goes into detail about all the family members from whom Jesus originates. Jesus' entire purpose was to come to be a Savior for the sins of mankind. What a divine assignment that was! God sacrificed His own Son to save you and me from all of the sins we have committed or will ever commit. That is a serious assignment.

The Angel Gabriel Visits Mary

Luke gives us another look at the story of Jesus' birth. He tells us about the angel Gabriel having a conversation with Mary (see Luke 1:26–38). Gabriel was sent (divinely dispatched) from God to bring her news of her upcoming pregnancy and the assignment of the child she would bear. "He shall be great, and shall be called the Son of the Highest: and the Lord God shall give unto him the throne of his father David: and he shall reign over the house of Jacob for ever; and of his kingdom there shall be no end" (verses 32–33).

Mary shared her concerns. She did not know how this could happen, because she had not known a man. The angel Gabriel shared with her that the Holy Spirit would come upon her, and the power of the Highest would overshadow her. He goes on to tell her the child she would bear would be called the Son of God.

Again, what must it have been like to have the news that she would literally be the biological mother of the Son of God? What amazing news she received about the divine assignment to which she and her Son were called!

Discovering your assignment can take place in several ways. No process is the same. Even identical twins must travel different paths. That is what makes us all special, and what makes our assignments so special. No one has your experience or your journey, so God communicates with you personally.

QUESTIONS TO
Ponder

1. Have you ever encountered or entertained angels but were unaware in the moment?
2. Has God spoken to you in the form of an angelic visitation? If so, what was your response?
3. Write down any specific instructions God gives you through the angelic visitations you encounter.

Prayer

for God to Send and Release Angels
to You to Release Your Assignment

FATHER, *I will always bless You, and Your praises will continually be in my mouth. You are Gibor, the God who rules and reigns over all of heaven and the earth. According to Your Word, You have given Your angels charge over me to watch over me as long as I live. When Your Word is spoken over my life, angels harken to the voice of Your Word concerning me.*

In Jesus' name, I ask You to release messenger angels to me to announce and clarify my assignment on earth, as it was with Mary, the mother of Jesus. In times when I may be fearful and do not feel qualified to do what You have chosen me to do, help me to surrender my will. Give me the confidence needed for my reply to always be, "Yes, be it unto me."

I stand on Your Word, which lets me know that having You on the inside of me is greater than anything that would attempt to come against me. I believe I can do all things through

Christ, who gives me the strength to finish my assignment. But I need Your help in those times when my faith is challenged. Lord, release a finisher's anointing upon me that gives me the strength to press toward the promise of the reward You have in store for me so that I will not settle for doing only part of my assignment. I thank You for releasing warring angels that destroy every plot of the evil one, who would attempt to delay answers to my prayers and derail my destiny. I am determined to keep the faith, to finish my course and to hear You say, "Well done faithful servant. Enter into the joy of the Lord." In Jesus' name, Amen.

STAGE 2

Development

Once you have discovered what your assignment is, you must develop it. I have seen some people receive their call and then immediately grab a microphone and begin ministering. Off they go! Nothing could be further from how the development process is supposed to go.

At age 24, I knew God had called me. As a matter of fact, I knew from a young age there was something special about me. I remember my grandmother rehearsing the story of how she knew the Lord had a special calling on my life. The same can be said for Valora. At an early age, she was preaching in Sunday school.

I remember one day as I was at church helping with the cleanup process, I talked about ministry to one of the deacons I called Uncle Nick. He made the statement that although you may be called at an early age, you still must take time to be developed. He went on to say there were certain processes every person must go through. At the time I did not quite understand, but as time went on, I slowly understood what he was referring to.

As I have lived life, there have been certain experiences I now value that have added so much to my ability to do my job as a sent one. During my early years I had zeal, but I lacked the knowledge to guide others through their processes. The wisdom Uncle Nick shared referred to the development process. Since I had not had time to be developed, I lacked maturity. He knew by experience that we all need both development and maturity to make rational decisions when we are faced with challenges and adversity.

Many times we know we are called, but we lack the development and refinement to walk with purpose. That lack makes it difficult to complete our assignments. When I look back to that day, even though I was excited about the work I would do for God, I realized I had no clue about what it would take to carry out my calling.

I think about myself and my process of development. I remember when I was a young boy at the age of fifteen or sixteen years old, I had dreams of growing up and having a family of my own. I remember watching my grandfather and saying to myself I was going to grow up and be like him one day. Although I had the desire, I lacked the maturity, character, knowledge, wisdom, experience and finances to provide for a family. Although I had all the attributes of a man and had all the physical characteristics of what a man looks like, I still lacked maturity in many areas. I walked like a man, had a deep masculine voice like a man and most people thought that at age fifteen or sixteen I was indeed a man. I did not, however, have the wherewithal to care for a family or the financial ability to provide for a family.

I further realize that my emotions and mindset were not very mature. I soon realized I was not ready for a family and needed much more maturity in many areas to fulfill my dream of having a family. I needed development that only time and living life could give me. There was no shortcut to my destiny of fulfilling my purpose and calling.

There are also no CliffsNotes or cheat sheets to go along with our process. Each of us must navigate our own path that is filled with ups and downs to arrive at our destination. There are no direct routes or paths that are devoid of challenges and problems. We must learn to navigate, overcome and master life. In fact, I now know that mastering life's processes is necessary to become fully mature.

I began to research the process and path that Paul, Jesus, David and Joseph followed as their calling was developed. None of them had a direct path to their pulpits of life. Their individual paths produced in them a passion for their calling and assignment.

From these men's lives, we find three elements within the process of development that we can apply to our lives. The first is calling, the second is consecration and the third is commissioning. Discovering and identifying our purpose is the calling. The development process is when we spend time to become defined in and master our calling. And deployment is the commissioning and releasing of our calling. Knowing and following these three simple steps can save us time, resources and heartache, and they can expedite the process of becoming mature in our calling. Here are these three steps reiterated:

- Calling: Identify and discover our purpose
- Consecration: Define and develop our ability to complete our assignment
- Commissioning: Release and deploy us into our purpose

One of the ways God develops us is helping us discover our passion. Once we have identified that one area or problem we believe we were born to alleviate, we will see our greatest fruit. As one of my dearest friends Sophia Ruffin has said, "Find your lane in life and kill it." Passion usually stems from something you love or something you hate.

Moses, for example, developed a passionate hatred for people being mistreated. One day while the Hebrews were working, an Egyptian taskmaster began to beat a Hebrew (see Exodus 2). As a result, Moses killed the Egyptian. His hatred was not directed toward the man. As far as the Bible records, Moses had never encountered this man prior to the day he killed him. His anger stemmed from the actions the man was displaying. Moses did not like the actions of the man; therefore, his fierce anger caused him to kill him.

Moses then escaped Egypt to the land of Midian. In time, Moses developed an entirely new life. One day while Moses was on Mount Sinai taking care of the flock of Jethro, his father-in-law, God called him for a specific mission. Moses was the perfect candidate to be dispatched to Egypt to tell Pharaoh to let His people go (see Exodus 3). Moses was passionate about people not being mistreated, he knew the people and the culture of Egypt and he could be dispatched with a message to free the Hebrew slaves from bondage. Moses had gone through a process that prepared him to be used by God to carry His message. The message was not Moses' message—it was God's. But because Moses was passionate about it, he could be used to carry and deliver it.

God then confirmed the word He dispatched to Moses with signs, wonders and miracles. When God sends you to carry and deliver a message, all of heaven and earth come into agreement to back you up. When Moses asked God who he should say was sending him, God told him to tell them, "I Am hath sent me unto you" (verse 14). Is it not great to know that when God sends you, He grants you the ability to operate with the full authority of heaven and earth? Moses interacted with Pharaoh on several occasions, and although Pharaoh did not want to release the children of Israel, he had no other choice in the end.

We must believe in God's sovereignty and in His ability to know exactly where we are on the timeline of our lives. I believe every challenge and trial we face is woven masterfully into the fabric of our lives. Two of God's attributes are His love and justice, and the difficult scenarios we encounter are guided by those attributes. As we navigate life's processes, we will find that every difficult situation we have encountered has been necessary to build us into the man or woman of God we need to be to fulfill our divine dispatch. God knows which ingredients are sent to build us up and which ingredients are needed to tear down aspects of our lives. I have always said our trials and storms do not have permission to destroy us, but they have been given instructions to usher us to the door of destiny and to drop off the experience, skills and grace we will require to complete our assignment.

6

Development
in the Life of Paul

The first of the biblical characters we will look at is the apostle Paul. Tracing Paul's life, we discover evidence of his developmental steps. After he is called on the Damascus Road and is consecrated as he spends time in Damascus, Syria, he is commissioned with Barnabas on his apostolic/missionary assignment (see Acts 13).

I am sure that at the time of Paul's calling to ministry he could not have imagined what his journey would be like. I am also sure that if anyone had told Paul what would befall him throughout his journey, he probably would have said, "No, thank you. You can keep it." In fact, I am sure you and I would agree that as we look back over our own lives, if we had known the challenges we would encounter en route to fulfilling our calling, we would not have chosen the same path.

In his letter to the Corinthian church, Paul recounts a portion of his life. I call it a part of his ministry résumé. He recalls his process, shares with us some of the highlights of his apostolic journey and recalls an extensive list of challenges he faced:

> Are they ministers of Christ? (I speak as a fool) I am more; in labours more abundant, in stripes above measure, in prisons more frequent, in deaths oft. Of the Jews five times received I forty stripes save one. Thrice was I beaten with rods, once was I stoned, thrice I suffered shipwreck, a night and a day I have been in the deep; In journeyings often, in perils of waters, in perils of robbers, in perils by mine own countrymen, in perils by the heathen, in perils in the city, in perils in the wilderness, in perils in the sea, in perils among false brethren; In weariness and painfulness, in watchings often, in hunger and thirst, in fastings often, in cold and nakedness. Beside those things that are without, that which cometh upon me daily, the care of all the churches. Who is weak, and I am not weak? who is offended, and I burn not?
>
> 2 Corinthians 11:23–29

I am sure this is only a highlight of what he faced as he heralded the message of Christ throughout the known world of his time. His process of development produced in him a far greater weight of glory. "For our light affliction, which is but for a moment, worketh for us a far more exceeding and eternal weight of glory" (2 Corinthians 4:17).

This is a statement you can only make from a place of maturity. It would be impossible to make this type of statement while in the middle of the tribulation that your development process is bringing you. He speaks of having gone through weariness, pain and hunger and realizing that they produced in him what comfort never could. Paul experienced betrayal at the hands of people into whom he had poured his life, he felt rejection from people for whom he wanted nothing but the best and he received wounds from people he never knew. Through it all, however, he learned to count it all joy. He learned that everything done in ministry must be done unto the glory of God.

Many times you will not receive a pat on the back or a thank-you for your hard work and dedication. What you will receive, though, is what Paul looked forward to—a crown of glory. The final appreciation comes from our Lord and Savior when He says, "Well done, you good and faithful servant. You have been faithful over a few things. I will make you ruler over many things" (Matthew 25:23 MEV).

We want to be able to say, as the apostle Paul said to his spiritual son Timothy, "I have fought a good fight, I have finished my course, and I have kept the faith" (2 Timothy 4:7 MEV). Imagine the sense of freedom and accomplishment Paul must have felt as he uttered those words to Timothy. These are the words of a life that has been committed to the work for which he started and because of the development he completed. I am not sure he could have spoken those words if he had not been committed to the process of development.

When Paul and Barnabas left Antioch of Syria and journeyed through Cyprus on their way to the Galatian churches, he was fully optimistic about his assignment. It is my belief that years later he was still optimistic. He penned these words in a letter to the Roman church. "And being fully persuaded that what God had promised, He was able to perform" (Romans 4:21 MEV). The words Paul uses in this context are *fully persuaded*. Paul's usage of these words signifies a maturity in God that can only have developed over a process of time. Patience, wisdom and strength are spiritual muscles that take time to develop.

Through his many adventures on his divine assignment, he developed and matured them all.

I am sure Paul wished he could give you the news that your divine dispatch will be filled with excitement, glitz, glamour, stages and platforms, but unfortunately nothing is further from the truth. We will experience challenges and tribulations. But be encouraged by remembering the words of Paul when he said this light affliction is working a far greater weight of glory. Glory is something that must be developed. The word *doxa* is the Greek word that is translated *glory*, and it means "honor."[1] Can we maintain our honor when things are going contrary for us? We will experience different processes that will help us develop our honor and the weightiness of the Lord.

Things like discouragement, rejection, betrayal, isolation, being enticed away and suffering are the marks of sent ones. The key is to learn to do all you do as unto the Lord. Some of the most well-known sent ones in the Bible encountered the same things, but they kept their assignment in perspective.

Paul makes a statement that many sent ones will readily identify with. "Let no man trouble me: for I bear in my body the marks of the Lord Jesus" (Galatians 6:17). He is declaring that he bears the marks of a sent one. Was he referencing a literal or a figurative term when he mentions his body? And what exactly did those marks look like? Would they resemble a scar? Were they battle wounds that reminded him of the many battles he had fought in the work of the Gospel? Were they emotional scars from the many people who had walked away from him as he attempted to disciple them? While we do not know for sure, I would answer yes to all these questions. Yes, they were physical marks that reminded him of the battle long after the war was over.

Many sent ones can identify with the apostle Paul. I can remember some of my own scars. I look at my right knee and the horizontal scar that reminds me of the time I was in the military stationed at Fort Hood, Texas, and one of my fellow soldiers and I were horseplaying in the motor pool. (If you are not familiar with military terms, the motor pool was where we parked our tanks and vehicles. And horseplay is slang for unsanctioned wrestling or fighting.)

As we wrestled and fought, my friend got the best of me, and my right knee was slammed against the ground. As a result, the skin was split wide open horizontally—all the way down to the bone. The blood began to pour out of it quite profusely, and I needed stitches. I am not sure which hurt the most, the pain of the initial bump against the ground, the pain of the stitches or the pain of walking around with the wound until it healed. Either way, all I can see now is the healed scar of a wound I received in 1994. This was 28 years ago. Although I cannot feel the pain anymore, the scar remains on my body.

Paul is very clear that the marks on his body were the marks of one who was owned and dispatched by Jesus. He acquired them in the process of doing what a sent one does. Paul was dispatched by the Holy Spirit on his first missionary journey (see Acts 13). He and his co-laborer, Barnabas, were sent to Asia Minor to spread the Gospel. Some received the message, but others did not. Some of the marks or wounds we receive come from being divinely dispatched into a world with a message that is rejected, unwanted or uninvited by many. You, too, will have scars if you choose to be one who is sent.

> From now on let no one trouble me [by making it necessary for me to justify my authority as an apostle, and the absolute truth of the gospel], for I bear on my body the branding-marks of Jesus [the wounds, scars, and other outward evidence of persecutions—these testify to His ownership of me].
>
> Galatians 6:17 AMP

Through his development process, he writes 13 of the 27 books of the New Testament. He leaves us a guideline for comparing the fruit of the Spirit and the works of the flesh (see Galatians 5). He also writes and gives us a thorough understanding of how to arm ourselves spiritually with the armor of God (see Ephesians 6). Paul's process for selecting leaders for eldership (bishops) and deacons is a blueprint for the New Testament Church (see 1 Timothy 3; Titus 1). In addition, much of the doctrine we teach on the prophetic and apostolic ministry stems from Paul's apostolic teaching to the New Testament Church.

Regarding the prophetic:

- Prophetic gifts (see 1 Corinthians 12:4–12; Ephesians 4:10–11)
- Prophecy in love (see 1 Corinthians 14:1)
- Purpose of New Testament prophecy (see 1 Corinthians 14:3)
- Prophecy according to faith level (see Romans 12:6)
- Prophets are subject to one another (see 1 Corinthians 14:32)

Regarding the apostolic:

- Jesus' apostles were ordained (see Luke 6:12–16; Matthew 10:1–4; Mark 3:13–19)
- Jesus' inner circle apostles (see Mark 5:37; 9:2; 14:33; Luke 8:51; 9:28; Matthew 17:1; 26:37)
- Apostles mentioned (see 1 Corinthians 12:28; Mark 6:30; John 21:15)
- Apostles sent (see John 20:21–22)

- Election of the apostle who took Judas' place (see Acts 1)
- Great Commission given to the apostles (see Matthew 28:16–20; Luke 24:45–53; Mark 16:15–20; Acts 1:6–8)

Paul's development process is a journey that has taught many leaders how to organize and develop their churches and ministries.

QUESTIONS TO
Ponder

1. Do you look at your service in the Kingdom as unto people or unto God?
2. Do you look at your scars/wounds as lessons learned or experiences to avoid in the future?
3. Do you look at your afflictions as working to create a far greater weight of glory for you?

7

Development in the Life of Jesus

*J*esus was the ultimate sent one. He received a divine dispatch from the Father. His life shows us how to deal with various challenges that are certain to arise because of the nature of our assignments. I will not say that we can trace any period of development in the life of Jesus, but we can extract from His life certain principles that can assist us in our own development as sent ones. Because Jesus is the ultimate sent one, we can pick out many principles. For the purposes of this book, I have chosen two that apply most to us. They are as follows:

- Jesus demonstrates with maturity how to deal with rejection.
- Jesus is the example of how to love everyone equally.

Jesus Shows Us an Example of How to Handle Rejection

I feel this is a major area for anyone to whom God has given a divine dispatch. Throughout the Bible, God sent His message through men, angels and His Spirit. Sometimes people will not receive what you are sent to say. This requires a level of maturity in your emotions and life in general. If you are moved by the approval, disapproval, acceptance or lack of acceptance of men, you will find yourself in a tough predicament. You cannot be sent by God and be a people pleaser or seek the affirmation and acceptance of men.

Several years ago when I was preaching a message, God gave me a prophetic word for someone in the room. At this time, I was somewhat new to receiving prophetic words. I continued to preach what I thought was my best message. The problem was that when I released the prophetic word, no one acknowledged it. I was discouraged because of the lack of response.

Immediately after I exited the pulpit, a young man came to me. He acknowledged that the word I had shared was for him. He said he had been apprehensive about coming forward because he was ashamed. This taught me a valuable lesson. I learned I can never hold back. I must be obedient to God and not be discouraged even when people do not acknowledge that something I shared was for them.

I will share another story from one of our mission trips. We were on foreign soil conducting a Gladiator Camp, which is a gathering where we train on the prophetic, spiritual warfare and intercession. At this camp, I preached the message. When I gave the altar call, people began to come forward. As I was praying for people, God gave me insight into the life of one of the young men who had responded. God revealed to me that there were some things this young man was doing in his relationship

76

that he was not proud of. He knew he had to change, but he had not yet taken the steps to change. As we prayed, I prompted him to repent for those things and not return to them. Just like the gentleman in my previous story, he had no reaction to our prayer time. He simply returned to his seat.

This time, I was not discouraged that he did not receive the word I had spoken. I knew the word had come from God. But I did have a problem with my interaction with him. The problem was that he was a big guy who had long dreadlocks. He looked like the kind of guy you did not want to offend or make mad. The truth is that while you will occasionally be sent to people who are receptive, more often than not you will be sent to tell people things they do not want to hear or receive.

At the end of the service, he came to me with his spouse. He shared that they had, in fact, been having problems and that every word I had spoken to him had been correct. He shared that when he left the altar he was overcome by uncontrollable tears. What if I had feared his stature, demeanor or appearance and refused to release to him the word of the Lord for his life? I had been divinely dispatched on a divine assignment, and he was part of that assignment.

God often sent prophetic spokesmen to deal with people who would not receive them. I am reminded of the text of Ezekiel wherein God says:

For thou art not sent to a people of a strange speech and of an hard language, but to the house of Israel; Not to many people of a strange speech and of an hard language, whose words thou canst not understand. Surely, had I sent thee to them, they would have hearkened unto thee. But the house of Israel will not hearken unto thee; for they will not hearken unto me: for all the house of Israel are impudent and hardhearted. Behold, I have made thy face strong against their faces, and thy forehead strong against their foreheads. As an adamant harder than flint have I made thy forehead: fear them not, neither be dismayed at their looks, though they be a rebellious house.

Ezekiel 3:5–9

Just like Ezekiel and Jesus, we follow a long line of prophetic spokesmen who have been sent from God. The text says God had to make Ezekiel strong against the people. That message is a key for us all. If people will not listen to God Himself, how much more will they not listen to you and me?

This still does not stop our responsibility to deliver the message. You and I will be sent to all kinds of people and places, and we must follow the example of Jesus and not hesitate to deliver the message we were dispatched to deliver. There is a warning in the Old Testament book of Ezekiel in which God sends a prophet to deliver a word. In this text, God gives instructions that I believe Jesus applied to His assignment, and we also must apply to our assignments—even unto the point of death. This text has been ingrained into my memory, and I think it should be ingrained into the minds of every sent one.

Son of man, I have made thee a watchman unto the house of Israel: therefore hear the word at my mouth, and give them warning from me. When I say unto the wicked, Thou shalt surely die; and thou givest him not warning, nor speakest to warn the wicked from his wicked way, to save his life; the same wicked man shall die in his iniquity; but his blood will I require at thine hand. Yet if thou warn the wicked, and he turn not from his wickedness, nor from his wicked way, he shall die in his iniquity; but thou hast delivered thy soul. Again, When a righteous man doth turn from his righteousness, and commit iniquity, and I lay a stumbling-block before him, he shall die: because thou hast not given him warning, he shall die in his sin, and his righteousness which he hath done shall not be remembered; but his blood will I require at thine hand. Nevertheless if thou warn the righteous man, that the righteous sin not, and he doth not sin, he shall surely live, because he is warned; also thou hast delivered thy soul.

Ezekiel 3:17–21

When God sends us on an assignment, we must know lives are at stake. People's destinies are on the line, and we are responsible for them. The important factor is not whether or not they receive a message, but our obedience to say exactly what God says in the way He says it. We can take this principle and apply it to prophetic words, healing or even deliverance.

Let's look further into Jesus' earthly ministry. Matthew records what happened when Jesus went to Nazareth, His hometown.

And when Jesus had finished these parables, he went away from there, and coming to his hometown he taught them in their synagogue, so that they were astonished, and said, "Where did this man get this wisdom and these mighty works? Is not this the carpenter's son? Is not his mother called Mary? And are not his brothers James and Joseph and Simon and Judas? And are not all his sisters with us? Where then did this man get all these things?" And they took offense at him. But Jesus said to them, "A prophet is not without honor except in his hometown and in his own household." And he did not do many mighty works there, because of their unbelief.

Matthew 13:53–58 ESV

The same anointing that was on Jesus' life to heal, teach and deliver was present in Nazareth as it was everywhere else; however, the text tells us He did not do many miracles because of their unbelief. It was not that they had not heard of the miracles or healings that had been done elsewhere. It was because they were looking at Jesus in the natural. They asked questions such as, "Is this not the carpenter's son?" "Isn't His mother named Mary?" "Aren't His brothers named Joseph, Simon and Judas and His sisters among us?" People can miss experiencing the anointing, ministry or deliverance they could receive because they look at us in our natural state and not as sent ones.

Allow me to share a snippet of my personal story. I am from a small town in Arkansas named West Helena, just outside of Memphis, Tennessee. It is quite impoverished socioeconomically—almost like the land that time forgot. My wife and I have traveled to over 100 cities in the United States and 29 foreign countries, but we have never been asked to preach in my hometown. Why? Because they are too familiar with me. They know me as Stephanie's brother, Nellie's grandson or Brenda's son. They have never really grasped the concept of me being a minister of the Gospel.

A few years ago, a relative of mine passed. After the funeral, we went to her house to gather as a family. One of my relatives was about to have a drink of alcohol, and he asked if I wanted a drink, too. I politely told him I would not be joining him because of my religious belief. It had been some thirty years since our youth, but I could tell it was challenging for him to see me grown up and being a minister. My relatives remembered me as John John, which was my nickname growing up since most people had no clue how to pronounce LaJun.

This was the same problem Jesus had in Nazareth. The anointing for healing and the miraculous was present, but they could not receive it because they were not looking from the correct lenses. When Jesus ordained His disciples as apostles and sent them out, He gave them instructions regarding how to deal with people's non-receptivity (see Matthew 10:5–15). He told them to shake the dust off their feet, and He pronounced prophetically that it would be worse for that town than it had been for Sodom and Gomorrah.

Jesus also faced rejection during the last week of His earthly ministry during what we call Passion Week. Jesus entered Jerusalem on His triumphal entry with all the people shouting "Hosannah! Hosannah! Glory to God in the highest!" In six days, those same people were yelling with the same enthusiasm, "Crucify Him! Crucify Him!" Jesus understood that His divine assignment was to come and live as an example, but then be crucified as a substitution and propitiation for all mankind. Unfortunately, He knew they would reject Him, His message and the salvation He came to deliver—but He remained faithful unto death.

People will change overnight—sometimes in a matter of seconds. This is one of the greatest lessons we can learn from Jesus. Never did He become bitter with people and their rejection of Him. Never did He ask His Father to dispatch angels to destroy them as His disciples wanted to do. He accepted their rejection and prayed for them. At the crucifixion, He looked down from the cross and gave us all a lesson on ultimate forgiveness. He prayed, "Father, forgive them; for they know not what they do" (Luke 23:34).

I wish that for you and me it would be different, but it will be just as it was for Jesus. There will be times when people will not receive us because their hearts are hardened and because they are walking in unbelief, but through it all, we must be faithful to our assignment—even unto death.

Jesus Is the Example of Loving Everyone Equally

Jesus loved everyone the same. Peter and Judas, for instance, both denied Jesus. He knew His responsibility was to love them, while their responsibility was to receive that love and respond accordingly. Jesus prophesied to each of them that they would betray Him, but He continued to love them despite what He knew prophetically they would do.

We learned earlier about the text in Luke 22 wherein Jesus prophetically declared to Peter that he would deny Him. In the same way, during the Last Supper, Jesus told Judas that he would betray Him (see Matthew 26:24–25). Judas even went as far as to ask Jesus if He was referring to him. Jesus is of few words and says, "So you say."

I recommend you read these passages again. I want you to notice that between the point where Jesus prophesies to them that they would betray and deny Him and the text in which they actually betrayed Him, Jesus does not change His demeanor toward them. He does not treat them any differently from any of the other disciples. He also does not distance Himself from them to protect Himself from the pain of betrayal. He knew what they would do, and yet He did not change the way He loved them.

I hope you have not experienced this in a church wherein a pastor treated people differently because he suspected they would betray him. When I was serving in the military, I also served a local ministry. When it was time for me to transition, the pastor began to distance himself from me. I now know it was because he loved and appreciated my assistance in the ministry. He later told me he knew I would be missed, and he was attempting to shield himself from the pain of losing another member who had served well.

Jesus had an amazing ability to love both saints and sinners equally. One day, Jesus was eating dinner at a Pharisee's home. A woman, who was a sinner, came up behind Him and began to wash His feet with her tears and hair (see Luke 7:38–50). Her reputation in and around the city was not the best. The

Pharisee began to say to himself, "If He is a prophet, He would know what kind of woman this is that touches Him."

Jesus addressed him immediately with a story to explain His reason for loving and accepting her. In doing so, He taught us yet another lesson on love. He pointed out to the host that from the time He had walked in, the Pharisee had not offered water for Him to wash His feet, as was the custom of the day. But this sinner had taken the time to wash and anoint His feet with all she had. I am sure the Pharisee's heart sank as Jesus gave this lesson on love equality.

We must ask ourselves, how would we have reacted? Would we have treated Peter differently from how we treated Judas? Do we show preferential treatment for those who are serving as part of our ministry, or do we treat people who say they feel led to leave the ministry differently? It takes a level of maturity to love people equally, especially if we disagree with what they said they heard God say.

Likewise, do we place a different type of love on those who sin? Are there different types of sin or categories of hell in our mind? Do we place people who tell lies in a different category from others we deem to have done worse things? If God sends us to them, will we serve them with the same enthusiasm? Will we go to the street or to the prison with equal enthusiasm? We must love all people the same. In God's eyes, they are all the same, except for the fact that they are either saved or unsaved.

If we serve in ministry long enough, we will experience some type of rejection. We will probably come in contact with people who have committed heinous crimes against society. We are not called to judge but to preach, pray and prophesy with them about salvation, deliverance and healing.

QUESTIONS TO
Ponder

1. Have you ever found yourself discouraged because someone did not receive the message God sent you to deliver? How can you overcome this discouragement?

2. Have you found yourself attempting to change a word from the Lord to make it more palatable for those to whom you were sent? If so, was it still effective?

3. Have you found some people to be less lovable because of their sin? Did it cause you to treat them differently? Why or why not? Search your heart and ask God to remove any preferential treatment or biased love.

4. Can you be obedient unto death as Jesus was? If He gives you instructions to deliver a word or to minister in a place where your life will be threatened, will you obey, even if it costs you your life?

PRAY THIS SHORT
Prayer

GOD, *give me the boldness I need to obey You, regardless of the consequences. Give me the same courage Jesus exemplified as He continued to operate in His assignment without being afraid. Give me the ability not to be moved to the right or the left when I am received or rejected by men—whether they praise me or want me dead.*

Lord, give me a heart to love people unconditionally, regardless of their sin nature or level of disobedience. I want to love people even when I know they will betray me and reject me. I pray for the ability never to change or compromise Your message to make it more palatable. I pray for the strength to complete my divine dispatch and stand before You one day and hear the words, "Well done, thou good and faithful servant." In Jesus' name, Amen.

8

Development
in the Life of David

*T*he next biblical character we will look at is David. David became the second king of the consolidated kingdom of Israel. Before he could wear the crown, he needed God to develop him. He needed to grow and mature so that when he received and wore the crown, people would respect and submit to him. It is often easy to give someone a title, but that does not guarantee they have the responsibility and character necessary to sustain it.

Here is what David's process did for him:

1. Prepared him to deal with rejection and jealousy (by using his family)
2. Taught him to fight and conquer (the bear, lion and Goliath)
3. Taught him to deal with the assassination attempt from a spiritual father (Saul)

4. Taught him how to deal with sheep and with discontented, distressed and indebted angry men in caves and in dark places

5. Taught him how to deal with people who did not understand his worship or assignment

6. Taught him how to deal with children who tried to kill him (Absalom)

7. Taught him how to deal with his own flesh and how not to make the same mistake repeatedly

The story of David's life begins in the book of 1 Samuel, with Samuel coming to David's father's house to select the next king for Israel (see 1 Samuel 16). Samuel was somewhat apprehensive, but the Lord reassured him that all would be well. Jesse brought all of his sons except David to the feast, because David was out in the field feeding the sheep. As sent ones, we will often experience rejection, especially from those closest to us. We will have to develop thick skin in these areas, because it can be painful not to be accepted by brothers and sisters. God had to allow David to become strong in dealing with their jealousy and rejection so that when it happened to him later in life it did not destroy him or hinder his momentum.

Next, David had to face external fights. "Your servant used to keep sheep for his father. And when there came a lion, or a bear, and took a lamb from the flock, I went after him and struck him and delivered it out of his mouth" (1 Samuel 17:34–35 ESV). We do not see the fight with David against the lion or the bear, but he remembers it during his fight with Goliath. "The LORD who delivered me from the paw of the lion and from the paw of the bear will deliver me from the hand of this Philistine" (verse 37 ESV).

The fights we face alone are the ones we will value the most. Goliath attempted to use his size and experience to intimidate

David. Unfortunately for Goliath, David had encountered intimidation and size before. He knew in whose strength he was fighting. "You come to me with a sword and with a spear and with a javelin, but I come to you in the name of the LORD of hosts, the God of the armies of Israel, whom you have defied" (verse 45 ESV).

My wife loves to watch the programs about the animal kingdom. I am not the greatest fan, but I will take time every now and then to watch. One of the things I notice about lions and bears is that their roar is loud and menacing. They know how to cause fear in their approach and their attack.

Goliath knew how to do this as well. He wanted David to know he had been fighting since he was a youth. Goliath represented a mighty warrior for the Philistines, but they did not know one of the names for David's God was Jehovah Gabor, which means mighty. David knew his God was mighty. He had seen Him defeat the lion and bear, so he knew He could do this, too. There would never be an enemy that could challenge the people of God that God could not defeat. This knowledge was where David put his hope.

I will extract a nugget from this story to say that as sent ones, many times we will encounter an obstacle or an enemy much larger than what we have the capacity to handle. But that obstacle is never too big for God. I can recall many obstacles I have faced, but none of them was a match for God.

David defeated all three obstacles, but those battles were nothing like the fight of an attempted assassination attack from a spiritual father (see 1 Samuel 24:11). David knew Saul was jealous of him and feared him being the next king on the throne. Although Saul was not present for the feast when Samuel came to coronate a new king, he would have heard about it. There was nothing that went on in his kingdom of which he did not have ears and eyes on the ground to inform him. And I am sure that as he interacted with David, he often compared himself to David.

Saul's own people compared him to David. At one point, a group of women chanted, "Saul has struck down his thousands, and David his ten thousands" (1 Samuel 18:7 ESV). This must have stirred up every jealous nerve in Saul. I counted at least ten times where Saul attempted to kill David, and each time the encounter taught David how to honor leadership—even when you have every right to kill or disrespect them.

- 1 Samuel 18:11—David is playing the lyre and Saul throws a spear at him
- 1 Samuel 19:1—Saul conspires with his son Jonathan
- 1 Samuel 19:10—David is playing the lyre and Saul tries again with a spear
- 1 Samuel 19:11—Saul sends men to David's house to kill him when he awakens; Michal (Saul's daughter) lets him down through a window
- 1 Samuel 19:20—Saul sent messengers to Naioth in Ramah and they prophesy
- 1 Samuel 19:23-24—Saul goes himself and ends up prophesying
- 1 Samuel 23:7-8—Saul summons the entire army together to Keilah to fight David
- 1 Samuel 24:2—Saul takes 3,000 to hunt David down, which really tests David's character
- 1 Samuel 24:4-22—David spares Saul, and Saul decrees his promotion
- 1 Samuel 26:2—Saul takes 3,000 chosen men to the wilderness of Ziph (David has the chance to destroy Saul but honors him in verse 10)

It is important for every sent one to observe how to honor people who dishonor you. It is easy to honor people who honor you, but when you must honor those who dishonor you, that requires another level of discipline and integrity. We do not honor people because they are always honorable, but because they are made in the image of God. We honor them even if they are not acting as if they are made in His image. We honor them because we are honorable. We honor them because we know they do not know any better. This is what David was learning as he honored Saul, even as Saul tried to kill him. This one lesson has produced much peace for me. It is incredibly important that every sent one learns this lesson.

Sent ones are often sent to rescue people, as David learned. We must be wise and strategic in leadership. The burden and assignment of teaching fathering to people who have never been fathered, or teaching the principle of honor to those who have never been taught honor, can be a daunting task. But as a king, David needed to know how to accomplish such tasks as those. As a sent one, you will also need to know how to honor.

David went into a cave with four hundred men who were in debt (see 1 Samuel 22:2). These four hundred men were David's first disciples. If you cannot disciple people who are distressed, in debt or discontented, you have not earned the right to be king. I know that is a very challenging statement, but it is true.

I can imagine that as these men were in a cave with David, they got into fights, were undisciplined and even smelled bad. David had to learn how to bring the best out of them. He had to get them to work together and fight together to win wars. They were angry, unruly and difficult to tame. But David had been training sheep. He had developed the skill of dealing with difficult, hardheaded animals, and now he got to practice it on people. God had trained David each step of the way for the next issue he would encounter. Each process prepared him to be a king. Each step was painful, but necessary.

You and I will need skills such as these because we are going to have to deal with people who are undisciplined. We will deal with people who are not good managers of their resources and with people who are angry. For some of the people who come to be discipled by you, life will have thrown everything at them. They will have come off the street and out of prisons. By the time they get to you, they want to do better, but they have never had anyone who cared enough to teach them to do better. They believe you can teach them to do better. It will be difficult, but you must remember that as a sent one, you have the solution for their lives. You are anointed to deal with tough situations and tough people.

David also dealt with people who had no clue about what he had been through and why he worshiped the way he did. David's life had not been easy, and it had required him to learn to worship unashamedly. Through it all, he always came out on top. God always caused him to triumph.

As the Israelites brought the Ark of the Covenant back to Israel, he celebrated and led worship (see 2 Samuel 6). As he danced, he danced right out of his clothes. At least that is what his wife thought. Let's hope this was an exaggeration of speech. At any rate, David did not shrink back when she characterized his behavior as dishonoring. He explained to her that God had called him, and he was dancing before the Lord. He would not change it one bit.

Sometimes people will not understand what you have been through. They were not there when your life was under attack and God saved you. They were not there when Saul tried to kill you ten times and it took everything you had not to fight back to defend yourself. They were not there when you were a young boy fighting the lion and God gave you strength to destroy it.

They were not there when God brought you through that last storm you knew should have taken you out.

Because of this, they do not get to dictate how you worship your God. If you worship until all your clothes fall off or your wig rolls off, so be it. But do not stop praising God! We must have the courage to learn that sometimes we have to allow others not to understand why we worship the way we do. They were not there, and they do not know.

I grew up with my grandmother in an old Baptist church in the country. When the choir would sing her favorite song, she would shake her head, and every now and then a tear would fall. She would let out this little shout that meant, "Lord, I thank You." I was not there to experience the nuances of her life. I do not understand, and I do not have to understand. And I do not get to dictate to anybody else the manner in which they praise their God for how good He has been to them. The lesson for every sent one is not to allow anyone to dictate when and where you worship. Do not let people place restrictions on your worship. At the end of the day, God is the only one who has always been there for you. Worship Him any way you like.

This next lesson David learned is, in my opinion, tougher than the others. David had to learn how to deal with his son trying to usurp his authority and take the kingdom. The Bible declares that Absalom, one of David's sons, led a conspiracy to take the throne (see 2 Samuel 15). Absalom was mad at how David had handled a specific situation. So many sons and daughters are upset with their fathers and mothers about how they handled something. They feel as if they would have handled a situation differently. The reality is, however, that without having been in the situation themselves, they do not know exactly how the situation should have been handled. It is arrogant to tell someone how you would have handled something that you have never had to handle.

Absalom felt David should have handled the situation with Amnon and Tamar differently. Amnon, Tamar and Absalom were siblings, but Amnon forced himself upon his sister (see 2 Samuel 13). Absalom took in Tamar to protect and take care of her, all the while believing his father, David, would enact justice on Amnon. David, however, had seen God's hand of mercy in his own life, so he did not deal harshly with Amnon. He knew God could have enacted justice on his behalf many times over the years, but He had not.

We all understand that Amnon was wrong for forcing himself upon his sister and that there should have been consequences, but what those consequences should have been, we cannot decide. We were not there; therefore, we cannot judge David on how he handled the situation. But David teaches us how to deal with what happens when our sons, whether natural or spiritual, turn away or are angry with us. David does the wise thing and walks away. He allowed God to fight his battle—and God did just that.

You will have those you have raised up and discipled turn their back on you, walk away from you and often try to destroy or take what you built. In those situations, you should do exactly as David did. Do not fight back, and trust God to fight for you. You do not need to answer them on social media—God has your back.

As a sent one, you must rely completely on God to know how and when to deal with your enemies, even if they are "frenemies." You do not have to defend yourself. God is training you to be a king or queen, and you have too much dignity to fight back or attempt to defend yourself. Although kings can fight for themselves, they have other people to guard them. In David's situation, Absalom was eventually killed, and David went back to Israel.

David's final lesson was learned as he battled his own flesh. One of the biggest scandals of David's life was when he had a relationship with a young lady he saw on a rooftop (see 2 Samuel 11). David was not supposed to have been at the palace—he should have been on the battlefield with his men. Had he been at war where other kings were, he would not have encountered her nakedness. On top of that, Bathsheba was the wife of another. When she became pregnant with David's child, he had her husband killed in battle. The lesson we can glean from this is that we should always be in the place where God has dispatched us. We should make it our goal to be in the place God wants us, as being out of place can be detrimental. As a sent one, you must always be in the right place.

I love David, because after he failed in this way, he did not fail in this manner again. While he coveted Bathsheba and sinned, he took his punishment and did not sin in that way again. In fact, when David got old, his servants brought a young woman to him to give him comfort. He, however, was not moved by her. He had learned his lesson. When he sinned by numbering the Israelite people, Gad came to confront him, and he repented (see 2 Samuel 24). He never numbered his people again. He learned from his lessons. We can learn from David's development process. We should always be in our designated place, and if we make a mistake, we should not ever make the same mistake twice.

9

Development in the Life of Joseph

One of the next biblical characters we will learn from on our path to developing ourselves for our divine dispatch is Joseph. The first biblical account of Joseph's life depicts him as a dreamer (see Genesis 37). He has a series of prophetic dreams that forecast the next years of his life. He has no clue he was only seeing the macro view of those events.

He had two distinct dreams. In the first one, he and his brothers were in a field binding sheaves, and their sheaves bowed to his. In the second one, the sun, the moon and eleven stars bowed to him. This might have seemed as if his future would be something glorious and something to envy. In fact, his brothers became jealous and envious of him instantly. If they had known the process Joseph would have to go through and what he would have to endure to see the manifestation of the dream, they probably would have cried. Nevertheless, it was all part of God's plan. For the next thirteen years, Joseph would have to live out the play-by-play of the development process that would help him acquire the character he would need to see the dream become a reality:

- Jealousy and envy at the hands of his brothers
- An assassination attempt by his brothers
- Transitioning from being a free man to being a prisoner owned by Midianites
- Being auctioned and sold to Potiphar
- Overcoming the sexual advances of his owner's wife
- Being wrongly accused by Potiphar's wife of sexual assault
- Being placed in prison
- Living life inside of prison
- Being forgotten about in the prison for two additional years after someone promised to remember him

One of the key things Joseph encountered early on was jealousy. I call it the Joseph Factor. It is when God favors you, but others hate your favor. I have heard quite a few preachers say that if they had been Joseph, they would not have shared their dreams. I am not sure I agree with this. What if telling the dream was a necessary catalyst to the other parts of his story, and those parts eventually created his process? I believe it was all necessary. If he had not encountered and endured every part of his journey, he would not have been prepared for his divine dispatch. The very thing God birthed him for was dependent upon him enduring his process.

You cannot avoid having people be envious of you. If you are called by God, you will encounter people who are jealous. People will be themselves, and that includes being insecure and feeling as if you have something they do not. If Joseph had not learned to deal with his brothers' jealousy, envy and insecurity of his favor in his father's house, what would he have done later when he encountered it? If his brothers were that jealous of the dream and the vision when it had not manifested yet, how much more would they be jealous of the reality of the manifestation of the dream?

In Joseph's initial dream, God spoke in types and symbols of what was to come. He showed Joseph having sheaves in a field and the sun, the moon and eleven stars bowing down to him. What would their reaction have been if they had been shown that Joseph would eventually become the vice regent of Egypt? None of them in their wildest imagination could have fathomed how God would promote Joseph to bless them.

His brothers were clearly jealous of the favor their father gave Joseph; however, I think it was the favor of God that they envied even more. If you remember the history of Joseph's story, you will remember he was a long-awaited son of his father. Jacob had thirteen children and Joseph was the twelfth. He was the child Jacob loved by the wife he had desired from the beginning. In the process of having his sons and daughters, Jacob had children by Leah, Leah's handmaid, Rachel's handmaid and eventually the wife of his desire. Joseph's life and destiny came with a hefty price.

The next step in the development process for Joseph involved a group of Midianite traders (see Genesis 37). This group was traveling near his family's farm, and his brothers took the opportunity to rid themselves of him and sold him to the Midianites for twenty pieces of silver. That was the price of betrayal for his brothers. When the Midianites arrived in Egypt, they sold him to Potiphar. Can you see how Joseph was in the process for a setup this entire time? Each time anyone made a move, it worked in his favor.

Although I am sure this journey was not Joseph's plan or his desire, nor did the process feel good to him, it was working together for his good. It was developing his trust in God and giving him a reassurance that no weapon that had been formed was authorized to prosper. It did not matter who was in charge on earth—God was still sovereign. Nothing could steal Joseph's prophetic promise. Everything had to work in conjunction with heaven's plan.

Joseph worked so diligently and with such excellence in Potiphar's house that Potiphar did not have a clue about what he even owned (see Genesis 39). Joseph experienced favor everywhere he found himself. One day Potiphar's wife desired Joseph, but Joseph maintained his integrity. She claimed he forced himself upon her, and Potiphar believed what she said. As a result, they put Joseph in jail. While residing in the jail, Joseph was placed in leadership. The favor of God does not care whether you are a prisoner or a slave. It is commanded to surround and bless you (see Psalm 5:11–12).

When Joseph went to prison, he was placed with the upper echelon of prisoners from the king's court. One evening, the chief butler and the Pharaoh's baker each had a dream. As a result, Joseph used his gift of interpreting dreams to explain what each of their dreams meant. His interpretation was accurate, as one of them was hanged and the other was restored.

The butler was restored, and he gave Joseph his word that he would remember him when he returned to his position beside Pharaoh. Even still, Joseph would spend an additional two years in jail. That was 730 days. Imagine sitting in prison waiting to be rescued and wondering each day if this would be the day—for 730 days. I am sure that at some point, Joseph began to doubt the dream of his youth would ever come to pass.

When we endure our process, we become the evidence that God is who He says He is. The enemy will always attempt to steal your evidence to discredit God. It is valuable, therefore, to share your testimony with others so that their faith is strengthened, and God will get the glory from it.

Every part of your process is the baton that passes you to the next level. Joseph's brothers devised a plan that set everything in motion. He was placed in the pit, and the pit passed him off to Potiphar's house. Potiphar's house passed him off to the prison, and the prison passed him off to the palace. Through it all, he came out victorious. If you do not endure the process, you weaken yourself. The process is designed to help you get where you need to go.

10

Development
in the Life of Peter

From the first day Peter met Jesus until the day Jesus was crucified, Peter underwent a process that helped develop and strengthen him for his divine assignment. The following are the processes Peter went through in order to be prepared for his assignment.

Peter probably received one of the most challenging prophetic words of all the twelve disciples. Jesus foretells what Peter's life would be like, and He reassures him that after he had gone through his sifting process, God would use him greatly in the lives of his brethren. But no one wants to hear the words, "The devil wants to sift you." I am sure Peter wanted to ask Jesus to take His prophecy back.

Have you had one of those moments in which someone shared something in your life that was yet to come, and all you wanted was to have the words taken back? I remember

Valora receiving a prophetic word that she would be given to hospitality. There were many days she wanted to call the person and say, "Take it back." Each of our processes is different, but God uses them all to help us prepare for our destiny.

As we have touched on already, Peter was told by Jesus that he would be sifted as wheat, and years later he wrote, "But the God of all grace, who hath called us unto his eternal glory by Christ Jesus, after that ye have suffered a while, make you perfect, stablish, strengthen, settle you" (1 Peter 5:10). Many times, I have looked at this text and not understood fully what Peter was attempting to articulate. What I have begun to see is that it seems to sum up the experience of his maturation process. Through three years of following Jesus and many years following the Holy Spirit after Jesus' ascension, Peter had grown and matured. This text was the culmination of many years of becoming the fullness of the man he only could have imagined when he first met Jesus.

I remember reading the text of Peter's life and watching him grow through his process. As Peter was fishing, for instance, Jesus instructed him to cast his nets again (see Luke 5:4–7). He explained to Jesus that they had fished all night long and had caught nothing. Peter was an experienced fisherman whose career had begun on the lake on which he was presently fishing. Still, Jesus gave him the instruction to try again.

This was more than an experiment in fishing—it was an exercise in faith. The lesson we can learn is that we can try again even after we have exhausted all our methods. We can try again even if our previous experience yielded nothing. Can you place your faith in God and believe for success? Peter submitted to the instruction of Jesus. As a result, "They caught a great number of fish, and their net was tearing. So they signaled to their partners in the other boat to come and help them" (verses 6–7 MEV).

I am sure Peter was quite surprised that he suddenly caught a great number of fish. The text goes on to tell us they filled both boats so fully that the boats began to sink, and they had to call for other boats. Imagine how Peter's faith must have grown as he witnessed the manifestation of the instruction of God in his life. God has the supernatural ability to cause your nets to be full. He can command the fish to get into the nets, and the fish must obey.

One experience can make a world of difference in our process of faith. There is nothing that could have taken that memory from Peter. Immediately after this experience, Peter fell at Jesus' feet and said, "Depart from me; for I am a sinful man" (verse 8). This one instance not only stretched Peter's faith, but it gave him a glimpse of his spiritual condition. He realized the gravity of his mortality and the enormity of Christ's immortality. This was the beginning of Peter's growing process.

Next, Peter was present as Jesus healed the woman with the issue of blood and as He resurrected Jairus' daughter (see Matthew 9). Each time Peter was able to witness the supernatural power of Jesus, his faith and his mindset grew. His belief in God's ability to use him to heal the sick and perform supernatural miracles grew.

This maturation process is critical to being able to complete your mission. I have seen many get a calling from God in a church service or conference, grab their spiritual briefcase and purchase business cards with their new title on it. But zeal without knowledge is damaging. So many gifted and talented but zealous and rambunctious young men and women have run headfirst into ministry only to find they lacked maturity to complete it well.

I always watch and listen to people's words. Their words can speak volumes concerning what is in their heart. Look at the words Peter speaks about the process of maturity.

According as his divine power hath given unto us all things that pertain unto life and godliness, through the knowledge of him that hath called us to glory and virtue: Whereby are given unto us exceeding great and precious promises: that by these ye might be partakers of the divine nature, having escaped the corruption that is in the world through lust.

And beside this, giving all diligence, add to your faith virtue; and to virtue knowledge; and to knowledge temperance; and to temperance patience; and to patience godliness; And to godliness brotherly kindness; and to brotherly kindness charity. For if these things be in you, and abound, they make you that ye shall neither be barren nor unfruitful in the knowledge of our Lord Jesus Christ. But he that lacketh these things is blind, and cannot see afar off, and hath forgotten that he was purged from his old sins.

2 Peter 1:3–9

I included the entire passage because I want you to see the fullness of the context. Peter is telling us that God has given us all things that pertain to life and godliness; furthermore, we have great promises from Him. We must grow in our knowledge of Him. This is the voice of wisdom speaking to all those who would read this aged wisdom. He says we are to diligently supplement our faith with virtue, and to virtue knowledge, and to knowledge temperance, and to temperance patience, and to patience godliness, and to godliness brotherly kindness and to brotherly kindness charity. He then seals his words with the following statement. "For if these things be in you, and abound, they make you that ye shall neither be barren nor unfruitful in the knowledge of our Lord Jesus Christ."

I am going to unpack this text a bit more, because I think Peter's experience gives us a wealth of knowledge we cannot easily pass by. Did you hear what he packed into verses five through seven? My grandmother used to say that an empty wagon makes a lot of noise. In other words, you do not have to use many words to say something significant. She would sit and listen to people speak, and if they used too many words, she would smile and say they needed to mature. She would simply say, "They talk too much!" In her experience, too many words meant a lack of maturity and a lack of wisdom. Oh, how I love the seasoned wisdom of my grandmother.

Peter says in verse four that there is a place in God wherein we begin to circumcise ourselves from the lust of the world and partake of the divine nature. I think this is essential, because if you remember in the introduction, we said that to fulfill our divine dispatch, we must be devoid of the desire to fulfill our own will. We must be desirous of the plan and purpose of God for our lives. My understanding of what Peter is saying is that it is not until you get to this point in your maturation process that you are really progressing. He begins to give us a recipe for success.

I remember preaching a sermon that used baking a cake as a guide. Often, we do not really know what goes into the process of baking a cake, but we know that several different ingredients combine to create something delicious. Using that illustration here, I believe we will learn a lot about Peter's experience. We will look at the ingredients of his life that combined to create maturity.

The first ingredient Peter mentions is *faith*. In the Bible, the word *faith* is translated from the Greek word *pistis*, which means "the conviction that God exists and is the creator and ruler of all things, the provider and bestower of eternal salvation through Christ."[1] This was why Peter had to learn the lesson while he was fishing. It was so much deeper than a fishing trip. Jesus took the opportunity to teach Peter and the other disciples a lesson on faith. We are to rely firmly on Jesus and all He is or says. If He tells us to cast our nets, that is what we are to do, because we believe in Him with our whole heart. Despite our experience, we trust Him and learn to obey Jesus without a second thought. As Peter said, "Nevertheless at thy word" (Luke 5:5).

I will share a story from my life to help you to see how important it is to have faith as a sent one on the journey of being divinely dispatched by God. A few years ago, Valora and I felt God was telling us to conduct Suddenly Conferences around the world. We wrote a book entitled *Sudden Breakthrough*, and from the principles within the book, we set up conferences to teach believers about prayer, fasting, giving, healing and deliverance. We also taught Scripture passages and confessions that we had seen facilitate breakthroughs. Through building up people's faith, we created the space for God to perform "suddenlies."

We had been to several cities throughout the country and a few international destinations. One day, a leader called and asked us to bring Suddenly to Little Rock. At first, I was extremely skeptical, because my experience had led me to believe Arkansas might be a rough place to conduct a conference. I had grown up in Arkansas, so I had seen firsthand the socioeconomic challenges people faced. I feared it would be difficult to receive enough in donations for the expenses the conferences required. As with any meeting, we believed God to produce the finances to take care of the facility rental and our speaker honorarium. I had the confidence in God that if He asked us to go somewhere, He would take care of the finances. Even though I had confidence in Him, I was a little nervous.

When we got to Little Rock, our ministry time was going well. Our offering, however, was a little beneath what we needed to make sure we could take care of all our responsibilities. When the speaker finished ministering on the last evening, I received a prophetic word from the Lord. In that word, He shared with me that He had sent someone to the meeting who was to sow a substantial seed, and He asked me to speak out His message. I was reluctant to speak, because I was a little concerned that maybe it was just my thoughts and not God's—but I obeyed God.

I stood and said, "God told me that someone here was sent to sow a specific amount of seed." Right after I spoke the amount of the seed, my wife said God had told her He had actually sent two people who would sow that amount of seed. Suddenly, two people stood up and said God told them to sow that exact amount.

Before this, I had not had the faith to stand and declare what God was saying, especially as it pertained to finances. This experience increased my faith. From that time, I have not hesitated to stand and declare boldly what God says to me. I am sharing this example because there will be times in which you will be dispatched to go to places where you may not feel God can provide for or protect you. Even in those situations, you must have faith that He has your back and will provide for your needs.

Peter's faith is the first of nine ingredients. Answer these questions before moving to the next section:

1. Do you firmly trust God and all He says?
2. Are there areas wherein you do not trust God?
3. Are there areas in which you struggle to trust Him? List them, pray about them and create declarations and confessions that help you overcome these areas.

He next says that we need to add to our maturity recipe an ingredient called *virtue*. The Greek word for *virtue* is *arete*, and it means "moral goodness, uprightness, a particular moral excellence, as modesty, purity."[2] At its heart, the word represents our motives. Why do we want to be in ministry, or why do we want the microphone? It is one thing for God to call us and choose us, but why do we want to accept the calling?

For the remainder of our lives, we must evaluate continually our motives, because if this ingredient is ever missing or gets skewed, we will become shipwrecked in our faith. Here are a few questions to think about:

1. Why do you want to accept the call to be dispatched?
2. Do you lack the moral excellence in your thoughts, feelings, actions or deeds?
3. What would you describe is your motive for doing what you do in ministry?
4. Make a list of your impure motives and pray about them until they are no longer an issue.

The next ingredient is *knowledge*. Its Greek root is *gnosis*, and this word means "moral wisdom, seen in the way we live our lives."[3] It is more than the knowledge of our brains that we can quote. It signifies a much deeper understanding. I have gone through seasons where my knowledge remained in the realm of "head knowledge." This refers to the knowledge that we have accumulated but that does not materialize in our day-to-day lives. We can say and quote all of the right things, but the knowledge does not change our lives.

The knowledge to which Peter is referring is much deeper than the passages we can quote but never actualize in our lives. It is time for Christians who can quote the Bible to get serious about how they are living their lives. Anyone can memorize a Bible verse, but living what he or she knows takes much more diligence. It takes discipline and obedience to live out biblical principles. I have seen drunk people who can quote the Bible, but their drunkenness is evidence they do not live what they are reciting. Let's answer a few questions to help us think deeper about this ingredient:

1. Are there areas in your life in which you have a knowledge of God and the Bible but struggle to live out the biblical principles?
2. Do you have a great vocabulary and mastery of the language of the Kingdom but lack the maturity to demonstrate it?
3. List these areas and be determined to master them.

We have now looked at three ingredients of our maturity cake recipe. The next ingredient is *temperance*. It is interesting to note that Paul placed this ingredient in his list of the fruit of the Spirit as he detailed his ingredients for a mature believer. Peter chose to use the Greek word *egkrateia*, which means "self-control."[4] It is further defined as the virtue of one who masters his desires and passions, especially his sensual appetites.

How often do we see people in ministry who have yet to master this area of their lives? The word *master* means "to become adept in, to conquer or overcome."[5] Because of the importance of mastery over our carnal appetites, a lifestyle of fasting is vital to maintain maturity. Whatever falls into the category of our appetite, whether it be desire for food, sex, greed, power or lust for more money, it must be brought under our control. We must also learn to control emotions, such as fear or anger, that are encompassed inside the pursuit of mastering temperance. To maintain our godly character and disposition, we must never lose our sobriety and self-discipline. Here are a few questions to ponder:

1. Are there areas in which you struggle to break free from carnality?
2. Are there areas you have not mastered in your mind or flesh?
3. Are you tempted by alcohol, sexual desire or other lusts of the flesh?
4. Are you still struggling with fear, anger or other areas?

Our next ingredient is *patience*, which comes from the Greek word *hypomonē*. This word means "steadfastness, constancy and endurance."[6] In the context of the New Testament, it is the characteristic of a man who has not swerved from his deliberate purpose and loyalty to faith and piety, even in the midst of the greatest trials and sufferings. Wow! What revelation this brings to the text. It is not just our ability to be patient with people, but it is also our internal attribute and quality of patience. Even though we endure trials and tribulations, we are not moved. We are like Isaiah when he says his face was fixed like a flint (see Isaiah 50:7) or Jesus when the text says His face was fixed (see Luke 9:51).

It was this ingredient that allowed Peter to trust in God later in life. It is told in Acts how Peter was resting as he was awaiting his execution in the morning and being guarded by four squads of soldiers (see Acts 12). The Bible says the Church was praying for Peter when an angel woke him up. By this point in his life, he had come to trust God and was not disturbed by the angel. Despite his current circumstances, he had faith that either God would rescue him or that it was, indeed, his time to die. He knew that nothing other than the divine will of God would happen to him.

The angel walked him out of the prison. When Peter arrived at the place where the Church was praying, they were amazed by the miracle they witnessed. This is the kind of patience we need when we receive our divine dispatch and are sent on an assignment from God. We need the kind of patience that causes us to continue going forward no matter what obstacles or challenges we face. This explanation gives us another level of understanding about our maturity in Christ. Think about these questions:

1. How did you react when you went through your last trial?
2. Were you constant in purpose despite your position in the process?
3. How can you position yourself differently so that the next time you encounter this same trial you will handle it differently?

Our next ingredient is *godliness*, which is an English word that is translated from the Greek word *eusebeia*. This word means "piety toward God, holiness, or respect."[7] This ingredient sounds simple, but it again forces us to examine our motives and heart condition.

When my hair was long enough to go to the barbershop, I would go in and have a seat to wait for my appointment. If other clients were in the barbershop, they would often use profanity. When the barber would call my name, he would say, "Hey, pastor, you are next." Instantly, the people who had been using profanity would apologize for their use of profanity. I would often marvel that they had more respect for me than for God, who had been there all the while.

Holiness cautions us to carry ourselves with reverence and respect, as if we are constantly in the presence of God. Sent ones who are on a dispatch from God and for God's purposes must continually carry themselves in a manner that is consistent with the nature of God's holiness.

Another analogy I can use comes from when I was a soldier in the military. When we were in uniform, we had standards we had to uphold. Regardless of where we were, we had to uphold the highest standards of military appearance and conduct. There was no place in which those standards did not apply, and we could be corrected by a soldier who felt we were not upholding that code of conduct. When you are a sent one with a divine dispatch, you must always keep yourself in alignment with holiness and the standards of God's image. Ask yourself these questions:

1. Do we only acknowledge God in the sanctuary or on holy ground?
2. Do we live a consecrated life regardless of where we are or who is with us?
3. Do we have parts of our life we hide from some people, or are we the same no matter where we are?
4. Are there disparities between what others see of us and what God's image of holiness is?

The next ingredient Peter adds to the list is *brotherly kindness*, which is the Greek word *philadelphia*. It speaks volumes to Peter, as it probably reminded him of one of his last lessons with Jesus. Shortly before Jesus' ascension, He appeared to Peter and the rest of the disciples (see John 21). At this encounter, Jesus asked Peter if he loved Him. Peter answered that he did love Him.

The finer details of the Greek language reveal a difference in what each man was communicating. Jesus asked Peter if he loved Him using the word *agape*. As Peter only understood love from a brotherly perspective, he answers that he did love Jesus using the word *philo*. The meaning of each of these words has a tremendous difference, although in the English language we use them interchangeably. We say we love everybody and everything.

I love Krispy Kreme donuts, for example, but I would not give my life for them. Jesus was asking for an *agape* love, which is "a tender love that is filled with good will."[8] Peter only understood love to the brotherly extent, which is the word *philo*. The ingredient Peter is trying to teach us through this story is that to truly understand one another, we must genuinely care for one another. We must be as interested in each other's assignment as we are in our own. This ingredient teaches us not to be selfish in our conduct.

Philadelphia is not just the City of Brotherly Love. It is the Christian attribute wherein we care for one another genuinely and authentically. If we possessed this characteristic more often in the Body of Christ, we would have more compassion one for another. This is the core of what we see in the book of Acts when all believers had all things in common (see Acts 2:44). When one believer was lacking, every believer pitched in and surrounded him or her to provide what was necessary. This value caused believers to sell land and personal items to make sure their brothers had what they needed. Consider these questions:

1. Do you think about the needs of your brothers or sisters, or do you just think about yourself?
2. Are your prayers and benevolence self-centered?
3. Are there areas in which you realize you must overcome selfishness and self-centeredness?

4. Make a list of areas in which the enemy fights with you to cause you to think only of yourself and your needs.

The last ingredient Peter includes in his list is *charity*. Charity is translated into English from the Greek as *agape*, which we defined above as a tender love that is filled with good will. This last character lesson was the thing he lacked when he was tested as Christ was being led to the cross. Do you remember when Jesus told Peter that before the cock crowed three times he would deny Him? Peter replied, "If I should die with thee, I will not deny thee in any wise" (Mark 14:31).

How quickly our words will be tested as sent ones on a mission for Christ. Only days later, Peter was tested, and he failed. The words Christ spoke concerning him came to pass. As Christ was being escorted away, a young girl identified Peter as one of the disciples of Christ. Peter denied even knowing Christ. Luke's gospel records that Jesus looked at Peter (see Luke 22:61).

I am sure this was not received by Peter as the best look, but, knowing who Jesus is, His look was still the look of love. I am sure Peter's heart sank as his mind replayed the scene in which Jesus told him he would betray Him. The same time this memory was being relived, he heard the cock's crow. If Peter had mastered this characteristic called charity (*agape*), he may not have only thought of himself. Seasoned and mature people who have a divine dispatch are not only concerned with themselves, but they are concerned about how their actions will have an impact on everyone around them.

I will share one more perspective on charity. The Bible tells the story of Ruth and Boaz in the book of Ruth. When Ruth was working in Boaz's field, she was allowed to gather grain from the corners. This practice was a custom in Israel. When a farmer harvested his crops, he would leave the corners untouched so that those who were less fortunate in the community could gather from his fields. This is the essence of the word charity. Farmers would automatically consider their brothers and sisters who may not have been doing as well as themselves. Ask yourself this last question: Do I love people to whom Christ sends me the way in which Christ loves them?

Peter closes out his recipe list of ingredients with a closing statement: "For if these things be in you, and abound, they make you that ye shall neither be barren nor unfruitful in the knowledge of our Lord Jesus Christ" (2 Peter 1:8). He encourages us not only to have them but to abound in them.

What amazing lessons we learn from observing the process of maturity in Peter's life. We learn that our development process is not only relegated to our oratory skills, revelation skills and gifting but also our character. Peter learned this over the process of his life. I am sure you have noticed people who have had amazing skills and gifts, but their character did not measure up. Peter's development process was quite eventful, but through it all Peter became the man of purpose he was predestined to be. And likewise, so will we.

For you and me, the process of development will be much the same as it was for Paul, Peter, Jesus, Joseph and David. God wants us to grow in maturity to the place wherein we have mastered not only our gifts, but also our character. He wants us to be a mastered instrument fit for the Master's use.

I was in the United States Army for thirteen years and was a drill instructor. I often say that you cannot send a soldier to war without having taken him or her through basic training. After a soldier has been sworn in, he or she must undergo ten weeks of basic training. The basic training is designed to teach every soldier the basics of military structure, protocol and procedures. This helps as they transition in and out of duty assignments. All military units function within somewhat the same basic protocols. In other words, they march and run in formation, salute, wear the uniform and do other things uniformly throughout the various units. No matter what Military Occupational Specialty (MOS) soldiers serve in, they have the same exact basic training program.

In this training process they undergo key components of being a soldier. These components include Drill and Ceremony, Basic Rifle Marksmanship, Land Navigation, understanding wearing the military uniform within regulations, Chemical Radioactive Biological and Nuclear readiness, and physical fitness to include running, road marching and hand-to-hand combat training. After completing basic training, all soldiers are shipped off to their Advanced Individual Training (AIT). In this training, they are prepared for what they will do while in the military (their assignment). There are over 190 different enlisted occupational specialties in the United States Army alone. Across the military forces—Army, Navy, Marine, Air Force, Coast Guard and Space Force—there are over 10,000 different military occupational specialties. Once they are done, they are sent (dispatched) to their initial duty station where they will join their unit and begin to learn and perfect their job skills.

If our military systems require such rigorous training, how much more should a sent one be prepared before they receive a divine dispatch? Immediately after we started our church, we developed the Discipleship Training Institute, because we realized a major part of our calling and purpose in ministry was to make disciples. Initially the course was designed for only people in our church, but now this course is open to anyone. The curriculum contains six core modules and lasts approximately ten months. Those modules include Discipleship, Biblical Interpretation, Christian Doctrine, Spiritual Warfare, Leadership and Homiletics.

In the Discipleship phase, we learn the process each of the disciples endured and where they ministered. During this phase, students learn to trace the steps of the early apostles and learn how to extract lessons from their lives. Biblical Interpretation navigates the first six years of biblical interpretation training I received from my bachelor's through master's level coursework. During this course, students learn the difference between the literal, figurative and symbolic meanings of Scripture.

During the Christian Doctrine phase, each student is taken through the ten fundamentals of Christian doctrine: theology—the study of God and His nature; Christology—the study of Christ; pneumatology—the study of the Holy Spirit; anthropology—the study of man and God's purpose for him; angelology—the study of angels; bibliology—the study of the Bible; hamartiology—the study of sin; soteriology—the study of salvation; ecclesiology—the study of the Church; and eschatology—the study of the last things as it pertains to God, His Kingdom and the earth.

After we complete the Christian Doctrine section, we study Spiritual Warfare. In this phase, we study the different enemies we will face as we journey through our time of deployment based on what Jesus and the other disciples encountered. During the Leadership phase, our students learn definitions of leadership and the basics of team development, goal setting and management of execution. They learn about the five leadership factors, which are the leader, the team, the vision, the plan and the execution of the plan. Finally, we study Homiletics, during which the student learns the parts of sermon structure and organization. From this foundation, our students can launch into whatever ministry they feel called to.

I pray your process of development is streamlined and you do not encounter many of the challenges that the sent ones who have gone before you have encountered on their divine dispatch. But the process is what develops us and matures us to fulfill our life's calling and ultimate destiny.

Never let anyone judge you, and do not compare your development process to another's. Everybody's development is designed to prepare them for their divine dispatch. People who judge you in one season of your life will be surprised that God was not finished with your story. It is all a part of the development process. Never allow one season, failure or anyone's judgment/opinion of you to stop you from believing what God said about you or what He sent you to do.

Every season of the process is necessary. In the natural, all of the seasons—summer, fall, spring and winter—are necessary; likewise, in life we will experience many seasons. They are all meant to prepare us to be the best we were destined to be. Although it may not feel or look good, keep going. Keep pressing, because nothing will be able to take you out before you complete your assignment in the earth. You will not stay in this stage of development forever. Here are a few thoughts to ponder as you navigate through your personal development journey:

1. David was still a king even when he was in the cave dealing with angry, frustrated, distressed and indebted men.
2. Joseph was the prime minister even when he was in the jail with an unfavorable charge.
3. Jacob was still a prince with God even when he was supplanting others.
4. Paul was an apostle even though he was killing Christians.
5. Peter was still chosen by Christ even though he denied Christ three times.

6. The same John Mark that Paul and Barnabas separated over in one season was the same John Mark whom Paul called for in another season.

Since we have taken the time to look through the lives of Christ Jesus, Paul, Peter, Joseph and David and observe what they learned, I would like to share what lessons I have processed in my development as a sent one.

The first thing I learned is that persistence, determination and endurance are mandatory character traits for a sent one. Situations arise frequently that will present you with the option to quit or give up. Sometimes others will try to get you to give in, but you must be determined to obey God and finish what you start.

No one is going to be more committed to your growth and assignment than you are. We often want to have people join us in our assignment, but I have learned that you cannot expect anyone to be more committed than you are. I have found that the life of a sent one is filled with life's challenges. But the one thing no one can take from you is your commitment and work ethic. You must be persistent and determined to the assignment Christ gave you. Every assignment will not be easy, and it will not be a walk in the park. I have learned that one of my greatest strengths is my tenacity and unwillingness to quit or throw in the towel.

A couple of years ago I went through one of the toughest times I probably could have gone through. One evening as I was relaxing with Valora and sitting in my La-Z-Boy recliner, I realized suddenly that I could not feel anything. I was attempting to move my arms and legs, but my body was not responding.

At this point, I was a little at a loss as to what was happening. I was only 48 and in decent shape. I rode my bike and walked daily. As my mind was racing, I was thinking, *What on earth could be happening to me?* My mind was also trying to tell my mouth to speak to my wife, but that part was not working, either. Eventually, I forced myself to stand up, and my wife could tell I was attempting to tell her something was wrong.

My wife had been a nurse for over 24 years, and she knew exactly what was happening to me. She also knew I did not have much time before what had occurred would prove to have irreparable damages. She did not tell me what was going on but calmly called the hospital. It felt as if the ambulance arrived in seconds. I am sure it was quite a bit longer, but it felt quick. The paramedic came in and began to ask me questions, such as who the president of the United States was and other easily known pieces of information. He also tried to have me explain what symptoms I was having and what I had experienced; however, I was not very coherent and could not articulate well.

I have heard my wife tell this story so much that I now know everything that was happening. At that moment, however, I could not articulate anything. I arrived at the hospital, and they began to conduct tests. What I was told afterward was that the doctor had determined I had suffered a stroke. A blood clot had gone to my brain and had cut off oxygen for a period long enough to cause a stroke. As a result, the doctor had to administer medication that, if he administered it quickly enough, would alter my condition. My wife gave the authorization, and they began to treat me.

After five days in the Intensive Care Unit, I began to recover enough to be released. My bills had accumulated to over $200,000. For the next six months, I was in speech therapy two times a day for five days a week. Initially, my cadence of speech was altered by the stroke. I sounded as if I was from Jamaica or somewhere in the islands.

I was also diagnosed with aphasia. In common terms, aphasia is when a blockage in the brain hinders memory functions. The way the doctor explained it to me was that it was as if I was trying to drive down a damaged road. If I needed to get to where I wanted to go, I would have to take alternate routes. This was how information in one part of my brain would have to get to other parts of my brain. It would have to take alternate routes to get there.

When the speech pathologist initially told me this, I thought about it for a day before I responded. The next time I spoke to her, I told her this was not acceptable. My brain would operate in the perfection in which God had created me. I would not accept her diagnosis. She, however, had been trained to look at the evidence and explain what it was saying. She did not know what to say to me. She had never met a sent one whose whole life had been dedicated to fulfilling assignments of the Lord, regardless of the circumstance.

The day I returned home from the hospital was a Friday night. Early Saturday morning, I asked my wife to text all our executive leadership team and ask them to come to the house. I waited until they were all in the living room, and I walked down the stairs to where they were sitting. I was still unable to talk at this time. They had never seen me in a position in which I had not been able to articulate my thoughts. I am a communicator, and it is what I do. To be unable to do it and do it well was quite unacceptable.

Several of the leadership team began to cry, and before we knew it, they were praying and decreeing over me that I would recover and that the process would be expedient. They began to plan for the next day, because it was Sunday, and I had been scheduled to speak. They decided that one of the associate pastors, Pastor Vinny, would stay at home with me while the rest of the team joined to support my wife as she spoke in my stead.

Sunday morning my wife got up and got dressed for service, while Pastor Vinny drove over to my house. I have only missed two services on a Sunday morning. I have either been attending or preaching somewhere in the last 20–25 years. Pastor Vinny later said I stood in front of the mirror pointing to myself and confessing and decreeing the Word of God over myself. He told me I came out of the bathroom and made decrees such as, "I will complete my assignment. I will walk again and talk again. My memory will work, and I will remember everything I'm supposed to remember." I do not remember standing in front of that mirror quoting anything, but Pastor Vinny said that he remembers it. As a matter of fact, he brought me to tears telling that story at my 49th birthday party.

I spent six months in speech therapy after my stroke, but most people never really knew the depth of brain trauma I sustained. I guess I made it look easy. I found my own rehabilitation in riding bicycles. I had begun to ride about six months before my stroke about twenty to thirty miles every Tuesday, Thursday and Saturday. After the stroke, every time I rode, I realized my speech became clearer, and my brain functioned better.

I became dedicated to getting better, because I knew my assignment was not over. I could have accepted the stroke and agreed with the doctor's diagnosis of my condition, or I could have agreed with God's decree that I was healed. I decided to agree with God. Before long, my doctor had to change my prognosis. It was not long after this point that the doctors released me from speech therapy. I was committed to recovering completely from what others had said I could not come back from.

During the first couple of weeks after the stroke, I had a conversation with God and Valora. I asked God if He was done using me to preach the Gospel and being sent to the nations of the world. I asked Valora this same question. Her answer was no. The Lord also answered that my assignment was not over. He told me I would write more books and travel to more nations. Since then, I have written three books besides the one you are now reading. Do not tell me God is not able to defy all the odds on your behalf. I do not believe He cannot turn a negative doctor's report into a positive one. When it comes to your assignment, you must not accept any other report than the Lord's.

We will all have those moments when life deals us its worst hand. But we must persevere, be determined and demonstrate our greatest endurance to see the miracle God has for us. Only God can use our most difficult situations and turn them around for our good.

One more of the greatest attributes of a sent one is the ability to reengineer yourself both verbally and spiritually. Valora and I have had to continually reengineer ourselves. You may have to learn new information and skills or practice with new technology. In this technological era, things change on a daily basis. You could have mastered one system, and by the next year it is old and antiquated.

A few years ago, for example, there was a social media platform called Periscope. For three years, we ministered within that platform and gained about 13,000 followers. We went live twice a day to tell others about Jesus. Before we knew it, the platform was gone. Twitter bought Periscope, and away it went. What were we to do? We had to learn how to build on platforms such as Facebook, Instagram and the newest platform called Clubhouse. Social media will come and go, but our ability to remain consistently relevant to our communities is a must.

Through it all, I have learned to trust God regardless of what I see with my natural eyes. What I see with them is subject to change at any moment. I also learned that no weapon formed against me and my assignment can prosper. It is illegal, and it is not allowed to prosper. It may form, but it cannot come to fruition. Lastly, I have learned to remain humble. No matter how many things God does and how He causes me to triumph, I have learned to be humble. Pride must die and remain dead.

STAGE 3

Deployment

The term *deployment* is a military term that means "the act of moving soldiers or weapons into a position where they are ready for military action," as well as "the act of using something effectively."[1] For a soldier, this word either brings excitement or anxiety. The excitement is determined by the length of the deployment as well as how many previous deployments the soldier has experienced. Anxiety can come if a soldier is not confident he or she is prepared for combat situations, or if he or she is going to be deployed for a long time.

Deployments can range from one week to over a year. An Army deployment can involve joining a field training exercise at the National Training Center in the Mojave Desert, going to the Joint Readiness Training Center deep in the swamps of Louisiana or participating in a full-scale military operation in some part of the world. I cannot remember how many deployments I went on during my time of service. What I do remember, though, is that each time I was deployed, I learned how to utilize and perfect my skills. We learned how to work better together and hone our skills to become experts in our craft.

This is what sent ones must work to do consistently and continually. People's lives are at stake. Others are depending on you and me to fulfill our destiny, calling, purpose and assignment. Just as I was ready to deploy after training for years, so must we be prepared to be deployed for the Kingdom.

For sent ones, our deployment phase is our opportunity to utilize the skills we were born with and for which we have trained. We utilize what we have discovered our core and distinct purposes are, along with what God has developed in us through our trials, tribulations and training, both formal and informal.

We put our training into effective action in the Kingdom. For the early sent ones, deployment meant being dispatched into the world of the early Roman empire to spread and advance the Gospel that Jesus had entrusted them with. For you and me, deployment means being fearless and boldly going into our modern world to see lives changed, impacted and transformed. This is the phase of our life in which we understand how we will be sent and what we are sent to do. Whether our assignment is in the Church or the marketplace, we are sent by God.

We understand that we are sent with resources, abilities, provision and protection. And we are divinely dispatched by God to preach, pray, prophesy, finance the Gospel, build the Kingdom, provide solutions, heal, deliver and set captives free. We are divinely dispatched into the world to represent Him in all aspects of His nature, character, mind and attributes demonstrating His power, favor and authority for redemption, healing, miracles and breakthrough.

11

Who Is Sent?

*N*ow that we have gained a better understanding of how we discover our assignment and how our passion for our assignment is developed, we will look at who receives a divine dispatch. When I looked throughout the Bible, I was amazed at how many times both the Old and New Testament used the word *sent*. In fact, in the King James translation, the word *sent* was used in a total of 664 verses. In some instances, God Himself was sending or dispatching someone, and in other cases people were sending each other for some purpose. In some cases, it was for official business, and in other cases it was more of a general sending.

As an example, the Bible uses the Hebrew word *shalach* to represent a sending away, and it often means "a general sending using to send, send out, sendeth and sent."[1] In some cases, however, translators used the word *shilluach*, which means "to send away or divorce."[2] When the translator uses this variation, it means God is releasing or divorcing someone (I will explain more about this meaning and context later in the chapter). In the New Testament, writers used the words *pempo* usually in a general sense and *apostello* in a more formal and official sending.

One might ask why I would take the time to go into such detail to explain that there are different uses for those being sent. I am glad you asked! My reason for differentiating is that some were sent on official duty and others were sent on more general assignments. It would be the difference between a mother sending her son to the store and a police dispatcher sending someone to check on a disturbance. Both persons are sent, and they are both under authority of the person who sent them, but their authority levels are much different. When a magistrate is sent to officiate business, the entire weight of the government is backing him or her up. Likewise, when you and I are sent on behalf of heaven on official business from God, all of heaven is backing us up. Every resource and every open door is released to help us fulfill the assignment.

You see, my friend, when God sends you on an assignment, you carry a unique level of authority. God sends you with all the forces and backup necessary to carry out the full assignment. When the president of the United States, for example, is sent to another country on a diplomatic mission, the United States Armed Forces travels along with him. On top of that, he has with him the United States Secret Service and any other special units necessary to accommodate his travel plans. When the president sends another staff member in his stead, they receive the same diplomatic status, protection and provision the president receives. That means:

Apostles are dispatched
Prophets are dispatched

130

Kings are dispatched
Evangelists are dispatched
Pastors are dispatched
Teachers are dispatched
Angels are dispatched

12

How Are We Sent?

When God dispatches us, He sends us out with power, authority, favor and support. Every believer has the power of God on the inside of them to bring healing, deliverance and freedom to others. We see this impartation when Jesus dispatched the disciples. "[He] gave them power and authority over all devils, and to cure diseases. And he sent them to preach the kingdom of God, and to heal the sick" (Luke 9:1–2). The Greek word for *power* here is *dynamis,* which means "the strength, ability, and power to perform miracles."[1] The word *authority* in the passage is translated from the Greek word *exousia,* which means "the ability or permission to command something to happen."[2]

We must operate by using the authority we have been given to release the power of God in those situations we want to change. The Bible gives an example of this supernatural phenomena as it tells the story of a lame man Peter and John healed. This is the same power through which we should operate.

> Now Peter and John went up together into the temple at the hour of prayer, being the ninth hour. And a certain man lame

from his mother's womb was carried, whom they laid daily at the gate of the temple which is called Beautiful, to ask alms of them that entered into the temple; who seeing Peter and John about to go into the temple asked an alms. And Peter, fastening his eyes upon him with John, said, Look on us. And he gave heed unto them, expecting to receive something of them. Then Peter said, Silver and gold have I none; but such as I have give I thee: In the name of Jesus Christ of Nazareth rise up and walk. And he took him by the right hand, and lifted him up: and immediately his feet and ankle bones received strength. And he leaping up stood, and walked, and entered with them into the temple, walking, and leaping, and praising God.

Acts 3:1–8

As this man begged for alms, Peter let him know he did not have money to give him; however, he assured him he possessed something else of immense value. He then used his authority and released God's power to manifest healing in the lame man's life. As Peter and John pulled him up, his legs and feet became strong. As he started jumping, dancing and praising God in the temple, the people inside marveled. They saw that the man they had known to be lame for so many years was now rejoicing. Peter made it clear that the lame man's healing was not a result of their power, but it occurred because Peter and John used their authority to release the power of God to heal this man (see Acts 3:12).

As sent ones, we do not have to beg God to heal—we command healing to manifest. Many are waiting to be set free of the bondages of sickness and all types of diseases. We have the authority to release God's power, and we must use it.

Not only are we dispatched with power and authority, but we are also sent by God with favor. I look at favor as having access to people, places and supplies that is made possible by the hand of God. Only God can give you favor with both Himself and with man. "So shalt thou find favour and good understanding in the sight of God and man. Trust in the LORD with all thine heart; and lean not unto thine own understanding" (Proverbs 3:4–5). We are not to reason about how things should be done, but acknowledge Him instead, and He will order our steps and direct our path.

A remarkable story of someone who was dispatched with favor for her assignment is Esther. This young Jewish girl was an orphan and was living with her cousin, Mordecai (see Esther 2). She became a candidate to be the king's wife after the king released his previous wife from her position. Esther did not come from wealth, nor was she of the same nationality as the other candidates. In other words, she was not qualified to be among the other women who were vying for the position to be the next queen.

But Esther found favor with the king and was chosen to be his queen. Little did she know God had sent her for such a time as that to be used to persuade her husband to save the Jews from the destruction ordered by Haman (see Esther 3–5). The hand of God protected her, and the favor of God gave her access to operate in and fulfill her assignment. It gave Esther the ability and the grace to do something she could not have accomplished on her own.

God's favor does not make us exempt from trials and storms; however, it does give us unnatural ability to achieve more than we could have imagined. Favor is not predicated on your education or your family background. When God releases His favor, it is oftentimes given to those who some would say are unworthy or undeserving. Favor will give an advantage to those who are the least likely, causing them to become the most likely to be chosen to do extraordinary things. God will dispatch you with power, authority and favor, and He will give you support.

You cannot do what God has assigned you to do alone. He will make sure you have the people, resources, finances and friends necessary for your success. Everything may not come all at once, but God is faithful to do it. You will not go on your mission alone. Even Jesus sent the disciples out in groups of two. Sometimes God will dispatch husband-and-wife teams, or He will use mentors to raise up mentees for support. Sent ones often work well with the support of people who move in the prophetic or who have evangelistic giftings.

My wife and I have always done ministry together. There have only been three times we have traveled to minister in separate places. As we have traveled extensively to minister the Gospel, God has had people in place both to support our journey as well as when we arrived.

As we were preparing for a trip on foreign soil to conduct a Suddenly Conference, two of our friends decided to travel with us and support us. We also knew someone who lived in that nation who came to assist us during the days we were there. This friend made sure that we were comfortable in our hotel, we had the supplies we needed, we had assistance at our product table and we were confident as we exchanged American dollars for the local currency. It helped immensely to have someone there who understood the culture and currency of the nation.

Our friends who traveled with us from the United States assisted in ministering with us. I remember that the first night of the conference we called people who needed prayer to the altar. About one hundred people came up. As we progressed through the crowd, it appeared as though the line would never end. What we did not know was there were as many people on the lower level of the church as there were in the main sanctuary, and they, too, started coming for prayer. My wife and I could not have prayed for all of those without being exhausted. It was a blessing to have other ministers with us that we trusted to lighten the load and pray for those who attended.

God had already prepared, positioned and dispatched our friends to support us even when we did not know how much we would need them. We just knew to say yes to the assignment God had given to us. We might not have always known how it would happen, but we have always known who would bring it to pass.

We can look at a vivid image of a mentor and mentee relationship in the lives of Elijah and Elisha (see 2 Kings 2). Elisha was willing to leave everything to follow Elijah everywhere he went. As a result of Elisha's faithfulness to his mentor, he received a double portion of Elijah's spirit and did twice as many miracles. Oftentimes, people want double portions of a blessing, but they are not willing to support and serve to receive it.

Apostles, prophets, pastors, teachers and evangelists work well in support of each other to advance the Kingdom. Apostles and prophets are the foundation upon which we build, grow and mature.

> Now therefore ye are no more strangers and foreigners, but fellowcitizens with the saints, and of the household of God; and are built upon the foundation of the apostles and prophets, Jesus Christ himself being the chief corner stone; in whom all the building fitly framed together groweth unto an holy temple in the Lord: in whom ye also are builded together for an habitation of God through the Spirit.
>
> Ephesians 2:19–22

Each of the ministry roles in the five-fold gifting is important and needed. None of these offices were designed to work without the other; therefore, they should never be isolated. The evangelist is assigned to bring in the lost to the house of

God. The pastor is the shepherd who leads, feeds and guides the sheep. The teacher makes biblical truths plain enough for the believer to grow and mature. The office of the prophet edifies, exhorts, challenges and comforts believers, and a prophet discerns demonic principalities that are attempting to destroy a ministry. The apostle works with all of them to establish order and to raise up other ministry gifts to advance the Kingdom.

Sent with Divine Protection

Although it is important for you to know there are enemies to your assignment, you should not be afraid of any of them. When God dispatches you with an assignment, He does not promise there will not be adversity. He does, however, promise to protect you from the hand of the enemy. He promises never to leave or forsake you. What an amazing promise that every sent one can receive. When we are given our divine dispatch, God is with us, and we will never go anywhere alone.

God is our refuge and a present help in time of trouble (see Psalm 46:1). He promises us, "No weapon that is formed against thee shall prosper" (Isaiah 54:17). In the Old Testament, God made a covenant with Abraham. Through that covenant, He established a relationship with the children of Israel. He promised to deliver them from the cruel bondage they were experiencing under Pharaoh's leadership in Egypt. He told them He would bring them into their Promised Land. Israel was chosen and dispatched into the world.

> Come now therefore, and I will send thee unto Pharaoh, that thou mayest bring forth my people the children of Israel out of Egypt. . . . And he said, Certainly I will be with thee; and this shall be a token unto thee, that I have sent thee: When thou hast brought forth the people out of Egypt, ye shall serve God upon

this mountain. .... And I have said, I will bring you up out of the affliction of Egypt unto the land of the Canaanites, and the Hittites, and the Amorites, and the Perizzites, and the Hivites, and the Jebusites, unto a land flowing with milk and honey.

Exodus 3:10–17

It did not matter what they encountered along the way to the land of promise—God protected them. Because their taskmaster, Pharaoh, did not adhere to the command of God spoken through Moses, God released ten plagues upon Egypt (see Exodus 7–13). All the while, He protected the children of Israel.

God first sent the plague of blood, where all the waters turned into blood. Second, He sent the plague of frogs that covered the land and entered Egyptians' houses. Third, God released lice that came from the dust of the earth. The fourth plague sent to the Egyptians was wild animals (or flies in many translations) that destroyed their land. Next came a pestilence that killed their livestock. After the pestilence, God sent boils that attacked Pharaoh, his servants and all of Egypt and their animals.

Pharaoh's heart was still hardened, so God continued with the seventh plague, which was fiery hail that destroyed their fields and trees. The eighth plague was locusts that ate all their crops and fruit. After that, darkness covered the land. Before God sent the last plague of death of the firstborn sons of the Egyptians and their cattle, He instructed the children of Israel to take a one-year-old male lamb or young goat without any defects and apply its blood to the two doorposts and above the doors of the houses. Doing this would cause the death angel to pass over their homes. This last plague caused Pharaoh to be willing to let the children of Israel go.

Even after Pharaoh released the Israelites, the Egyptians still pursued them. The Israelites found themselves in the midst of quite a challenge. The Egyptians were closing in behind them, and the Red Sea was in front of them. God again protected them by opening the Red Sea. He caused the waters to part as Moses commanded, which allowed the Israelites to cross the Red Sea on dry land. But as the Egyptians got in the middle of the Red Sea, God caused the sea to close. This resulted in killing all who were coming to bring harm upon His chosen people.

No matter what the children of Israel faced that was meant to harm them or keep them in bondage, they were able to be victorious. Nothing was able to stop them from getting to the land of promise that flowed with milk and honey. God will get you to the place He promised by any means necessary.

You will not succumb to the desires of the enemy. God is Jehovah Rohi; He is your Shepherd.[3] A shepherd knows how to protect his sheep from the enemy who desires to destroy them. He will lead them in the way they should go. The 23rd Psalm gives us a vivid picture of the responsibility of our Shepherd and His faithfulness toward us.

The LORD is my shepherd; I shall not want. He maketh me to lie down in green pastures: he leadeth me beside the still waters. He restoreth my soul: he leadeth me in the paths of righteousness for his name's sake. Yea, though I walk through the valley of the shadow of death, I will fear no evil: for thou art with me; thy rod and thy staff they comfort me. Thou preparest a table before me in the presence of mine enemies: thou anointest my head with oil; my cup runneth over. Surely goodness and mercy shall follow me all the days of my life: and I will dwell in the house of the LORD for ever.

When I think about God's divine protection, I think about the three Hebrew boys, Shadrach, Meshach and Abednego (see Daniel 3). These young men were dispatched to be examples of the importance of always serving the true and living God. They refused to bow to the golden image belonging to King Nebuchadnezzar. In the king's disapproval of their refusal to bow, he threatened to throw them in a fiery furnace.

Do you think that if most people were forced to choose between bowing to another god or being thrown into a fire they would make the same choice? Would you take a stand on your belief that Jehovah is the true and living God? Would you commit not to serve another, even if it meant death? One thing these three young men were certain of was God's ability to protect them. King Nebuchadnezzar's rule to bow to his golden image did not move the young men, even when facing his threat to throw them in the fiery furnace. It did not deter them when the temperature of the furnace was raised seven times hotter than it was initially. I love their response:

> If it be so, our God whom we serve is able to deliver us from the burning fiery furnace, and he will deliver us out of thine hand, O king. But if not, be it known unto thee, O king, that we will not serve thy gods, nor worship the golden image which thou hast set up.
>
> Daniel 3:17–18

God proved to be faithful to protect these men from the imminent death of the fiery furnace when even the men who threw them into the furnace were consumed from the fire. As a result of their obedience, God was able to perform a miracle that could not be denied. Even though the king's men threw only three men into the furnace, a fourth man showed up. As a result, the king acknowledged publicly this phenomenon.

> Therefore I make a decree, That every people, nation, and language, which speak any thing amiss against the God of Shadrach,

Meshach, and Abednego, shall be cut in pieces, and their houses shall be made a dunghill: because there is no other God that can deliver after this sort.

Daniel 3:29

The hand of God on your life will make even your enemies change their minds and begin to serve the God you serve. Even when the weapon is formed, it cannot prosper.

God's divine protection is not exclusively about the sent ones who have been dispatched. It is also about what they carry inside of them and the assignment they have been given to complete. Despite adversity, you will arrive at your destination because God is faithful to bring His will to pass.

Sent with Divine Provision

When God dispatches you to an assignment, He has already provided everything you need to accomplish the task. As you operate in the grace of your ministry, you may not always clearly see the provision. Each journey requires you to walk by faith and not by sight. Everything is accessed by faith. You first must hear the voice of God, and then you must make the decision to go where He has called.

Your obedience to do what God has asked you to do cannot be contingent upon whether or not you see the provision in the natural. You go because you have a firm, relying trust in Jehovah Jireh. He has already supplied your needs according to His riches in glory—not according to what your financial status is. God does not want you to worry about whether or not you will have the provision you need.

Jesus tells us not to worry about what we are going to eat or drink or what we will wear (see Matthew 6:25). Our primary focus must be seeking the Kingdom of God and its righteousness. "But seek ye first the kingdom of God, and his righteousness; and all these things shall be added unto you" (Matthew 6:33). God already knows what you have need of and has already provided. As Matthew says, when we seek Him first, everything else will be given to us.

We see the provision of God for food, raiment, shelter and money throughout the Bible. The prophet Elijah, for instance, was told to go to the brook Cherith where the ravens would provide for him (see 1 Kings 17). He remained by the brook, and the ravens fed him evening and morning. Even though the raven by nature is a scavenger, God directed it to bring Elijah sustainable food. God can give instructions to make provision for you out of the ordinary nature of things.

I remember Valora telling the story of the provision she received when she was planning to attend college for nursing. She had applied to and had been accepted at Howard University in Washington, DC. During this time, her stepfather was the caretaker for a gentleman. I am not sure how this man heard about what her plans were, but one day he asked her to come see him. He shared with her that if she decided to go to a local college, he would pay for her schooling and books.

God already knows what we need, and He has assigned people in the earth to provide it—especially when it is for an assignment He has dispatched you to complete. Valora always says, "Whenever God sends you somewhere, you never have enough money or people." That is where God steps in.

Let's look at the story of Elisha and the widow woman who had two sons (see 2 Kings 4). The woman went to the prophet and pleaded with him to help her. She told him a creditor was coming to take her two sons to pay off a debt she could not repay. She was a widow and had no means or way of providing for herself, and the law allowed creditors to take the children of the ones in debt as slaves if they could not pay off a debt.

The prophet asked her what was in her house. She told him nothing except some oil. Elisha then instructed her to borrow vessels into which she could pour the oil. She did as the prophet instructed, and her oil continued to flow until she ran out of vessels. She went back to the prophet, and he told her to sell the oil to pay her creditors and live on the rest. God is aware of when He needs to intervene to supernaturally provide for us. It is what He does best. We serve a supernatural God whose ability to provide for us is not limited by what we can see.

Remember that God is omnipotent and omniscient, which means that when He commands, He already knows the location of the thing for which we have need. When money was needed to pay the temple tax, for instance, Jesus told Peter to drop a fishing line. "Take the first fish that comes up. And when you open its mouth, you will find a coin. Take it and give it to them for you and Me" (Matthew 17:27 MEV). God provided supernaturally for their natural needs. Scripture is filled with stories of the supernatural power of God as He provided for His people.

Our church was looking to purchase a building; however, the sale of the building did not go as we planned due to no fault of our own. We looked all over the city of Tampa and could not find a location. One day during our search, I had my administrator call a Realtor about a specific property. The Realtor said they could not have a church in the property about which we were enquiring, but she shared that she did have a place that would be perfect. We looked at it and felt it would work perfectly for our needs.

Our first day in the new facility, we knew we would need more chairs. I received and shared a prophecy that someone would walk up after service and donate the money for the seating we needed—and that donation came in. As we were processing the donation with the bank, we realized one of our credit processors connected to our app had not made a deposit in twenty months. If the member's donation had processed quickly, we would not have looked into our finances, and we would not have seen the missing revenue. We had not missed the money, because we have always been extremely blessed financially. Guess what the amount was for the pending deposits for twenty months. Over $85,000! God had a secret savings plan for us all that time, and He knew when and how to release it. It was our money already.

You cannot tell me God is not a supernatural provider. He revealed to us the hidden money at the exact time we needed finances for the equipment for our new building. Do not ever doubt God and His ability to provide for a journey He has dispatched you to do. God promises to always provide for us when He dispatches us somewhere for Kingdom business. Never worry or fret, but trust that where He sends you, He will provide.

13

What Are We Sent to Do?

Each of us was born with a distinct purpose. No one has the exact same purpose or path in life.

One day, as I sat at the top of a restaurant in Mobile, Alabama, I began to watch the cars on the interstate below. The place where I was standing gave me a view of two roads that ran through downtown Mobile. One of the roads was I-10. If you traveled to the west, you would end up eventually in California. If you drove on it to the east, you would end up eventually in Jacksonville, Florida. The other road was I-65, and it had a north and south route that started in Mobile and eventually led to Chicago, Illinois.

As I watched these two interstates, I was amazed at all the different vehicles on the road that were traveling in many different directions with many different purposes. I could also see the ships in the Bay of Mobile loading and unloading cargo from all around the world. Simultaneously, I could see flights taking off and landing at Mobile International Airport. All these automobiles, trucks and ships had been dispatched. They all had somewhere to go because someone needed what was in them.

Those vehicles being dispatched are like our lives. Someone needs what we carry, and they have requested it from God. He is about to dispatch us to deliver it.

Sent to Set the Captives Free and Bring Deliverance

We are dispatched to set the captives free. Some people are bound by tradition and religion, while others are bound by addictions and systems of men. In some way, shape or form, we are all dealing with something.

A few years ago, my wife and I had the opportunity to go to Trinidad for the first time. We landed in Port of Spain and adjusted quickly to the way things were conducted. There was, however, one thing that kept bothering me. To some degree, I felt as if the people were bound and could not get free.

I had studied religion at the University of South Florida, and as part of those studies, I took courses on the different religions of the world. Trinidad was one of those countries in which there was much religious syncretism. The word *syncretism* means, "the combination of different forms of belief or practice."[1] People can have several religious systems in their family line, and they are taught to deal with them together. That is what syncretism boils down to. One young lady could be Trinidadian, for example, while her mother is Chinese and her father is Indian. What if she married a Trinidadian whose family is from Africa? Can you see the challenge here?

I will go a little deeper into our scenario. What if her mother was Buddhist and her father Hindu, but his family practiced the religions of their fathers, which was Yoruba? Now they are Christian, and they try to marry all those religious beliefs into one. It seems impossible to do, but many times people are trying to intermingle all their religious beliefs together.

This was what I was feeling, and I could not shake it loose. People were trying desperately to obtain their breakthrough, but they were entangled with so many different religions that it was impossible. I did not realize this dynamic when we agreed to go on the mission trip, but the complicated system of faith created one of the toughest trips of all of them.

We put on a Gladiator Camp, and when we started to minister, I could feel the spirits of the mixture of religious belief systems in the atmosphere. The place where we were ministering held 400 upstairs and around 200 to 300 downstairs. I knew God would do something great. A friend and his wife were traveling with us, but that was all who made up our team. We only had a team of four, but we were looking at 400 to 600 people to whom we were to minister.

As always, the people were really excited for the prophetic and intercession ministry, but when it came time for the deliverance ministry, they were uneasy. I knew by experience this meant we were really going to help people become free. When we started to pray for people individually, they came from all over the building. Once we finished praying for the people upstairs, we began praying for the people downstairs. I looked at my friend and asked him where all the people were coming from. We laughed and kept ministering. By the time the evening was over, many people were free. We have photos from this meeting that show how many people were in line for the altar because they wanted to be free.

In Mark 5, Jesus got on a boat and traveled to an area called the Gerasenes. When He got off the boat, He encountered a demon-possessed man who was cutting himself and living in the tombs. He was uncontrollable, even when restrained by chains. No one wanted to be around him. Every time some-one tried to place him in restraints, he tore them apart. Jesus looked at him and knew exactly what was happening to him.

No one wants to be bound or live in caves or cemeteries. People do not like to live like this. This man was cutting himself because he wanted to get the demons out of him. He did not want them inside him, and he thought cutting himself would alleviate the pain.

Jesus approached him and asked him his name. A demon within the young man answered and said his name was Le-gion. I am sure the demon who answered was only the leader, or he was the demon who had taken the position of authority and was speaking for the other demons inside the man. Using the name Legion meant that 6,000 demons were inside one man.[2] No wonder he was schizophrenic and did not know if he wanted to live in caves or the cemetery. The demons asked Jesus not to torment them. For them, tormenting meant cast-ing them out of the man. That is exactly what Jesus did. He cast them out. Why? Because you cannot counsel demons or starve them out. You must cast them out and command them to go.

The demons ran out of the man and went into swine graz-ing nearby. Off the cliff they went. Again, with that many de-mons inside them, they probably did not know which way they wanted to go. The man was now free. I can only imagine what it felt like for the man to feel free in his mind, free in his body and free in his emotions. No racing thoughts or double mindedness, no competing thoughts in his mind. He came and fell at Jesus' feet. He wanted to be around this man forever; however, Jesus had another assignment.

Trying to help people receive freedom is one of the jobs of a sent one. God dispatches sent ones to go and set the captives free. The enemy has held them hostage in their mind, will, emotions and flesh. In some area of their life, they have opened the door to demons, and they must get the peace a sent one brings. Our decree is that they shall be free.

I remember another time we were doing the same kind of meeting in Orlando. I was teaching, and it was nearing lunchtime. I remember, because the entire team went to lunch while I remained in the sanctuary to minister deliverance to a young lady. As I was ministering to her, I heard the Lord say I should call out the demons of perversion. I began to tell them they needed to leave this young woman. While she was being delivered of most of them, one decided it did not want to come out. I continued to command one after another out until she was free.

Later, she did a video for a Fearless Challenge[3] event my wife was conducting. In that video, she shared that she had been a victim of sex trafficking. For ten years, she had been forced to have sex with multiple men a day. I cannot imagine how that must have felt. I cannot imagine how that level of bondage, spiritual wickedness and demonic possession must have wreaked havoc in her life. She still gives us credit and appreciation for helping her receive freedom.

We are sent to go in like spiritual SWAT[4] teams who help loose captives who are bound. I am so happy when I see people receive freedom and deliverance from Satan's grip. I pray you will receive the boldness to go and set the captives free. You will command spirits to go. You will set people free. You will not be afraid of the demons, but you will be bold and command them to go in Jesus' name. You will see people healed from the possession and oppression that only comes from the devil and his cohorts. You are sent to set the captives free. Many will come to Jesus because of your work helping people get free and stay free.

Sent to Bring Healing

We are dispatched with a message and anointing of healing. The Bible shares with us what Christ's final instruction to His disciples was: "They shall lay hands on the sick, and they shall recover" (Mark 16:18). This message still applies to sent ones today. God will dispatch you to provide healing. He will send you to places you have never heard of to release healing to people who may have not been able to receive it otherwise. "Is any sick among you? let him call for the elders of the church; and let them pray over him, anointing him with oil in the name of the Lord: and the prayer of faith shall save the sick, and the Lord shall raise him up" (James 5:14–15). The passage goes on to say that the effectual prayer of the righteous avails much.

Your prayers have much power, so never doubt when God asks you to pray for someone—they shall be healed. God also grants prayer petitions of faith. I believe God grants healing, not just in places where someone has a special gift of healing and miracles, but also where someone believes with all his or her heart.

There have been several times He sent us to heal, and God Himself performed great miracles. My first miracle of healing was in 1996 when I was stationed in Schofield Barrack, Hawaii. I received a phone call that my grandmother had been admitted into the hospital. My grandmother had raised me from the age of two months old, and she was near and dear to my heart. They explained she might not live long, because she had experienced a heart attack and two strokes. I began an absolute fast (no water or food) because I knew that when I arrived, I would need power and faith.

Smith Wigglesworth was a British evangelist who moved in the miraculous and brought healing to many. I had been reading a few of Wigglesworth's books on fasting and prayer.[5]

I quickly processed my leave request and boarded an airplane for Memphis, Tennessee, where my grandmother was.

When I landed, my older sister picked me up and told me to brace myself, because my grandmother did not look good. She was in the Intensive Care Unit of the hospital. When I walked into the ICU, I could not tell who she was. Her face was swollen terribly, and she was in a coma. I could not believe this was her.

I had to take a minute to walk back outside of the room and gather myself. I prayed and asked God for the courage and strength to go back and be the prayer warrior she needed me to be. When I returned to her side, I grabbed her hand and spoke to her. She squeezed my hand. I knew she recognized I was there and that her son had come to see her. I prayed passionately for her at that moment. I declared that she was healed and that she would fully recover. I anointed her with oil. In fourteen days, she was out of the coma, out of the hospital bed, recovered and walking as if nothing had been wrong with her. I believe in the power of prayer and in God's ability to heal—she was the one who taught me.

When I was a little boy, about seven or eight, I got chicken-pox over the Thanksgiving holiday. I did everything my grand-mother told me *not* to do. She told me not to scratch the bumps, and I did. Then she told me not to spread water on them, and I did. Before you knew it, I had a bunch of scabbed sores all over. The one I was most affected by was the one in my mouth that prevented me from eating.

I remember asking her if I could eat the Thanksgiving meal. Like everyone else, I believed my grandmother cooked the best sweet potato pies. (In fact, I still make her sweet potato pies at Thanksgiving, and everyone loves them.) That Thanksgiving evening, I really wanted to eat, but the scabs were covering my mouth. Every time I would try to eat, they would tear.

If I did not receive healing, I could not eat. So, I prayed a simple prayer. *Lord, please let me be healed so that I can eat.* Yes, I know it was selfish, but I wanted to eat! Guess what? God answered my prayer. The scabs came off. When my grandmother asked me what happened, I told her that I had wanted to eat, so I prayed and asked God, and He answered me. I had the most memorable Thanksgiving meal that year. From that time, my grandmother always told everyone about the time I prayed and asked God to heal me and He had. Healing is that simple. God wants to send you to bring healing to others.

We had a friend who had been in a traffic accident. Since he had been driving at a high rate of speed, his injuries were extensive. It did not look as if he would live. My wife and I took a couple of days to pray and fast, and then we drove to the hospital. I remember walking into his room and seeing him connected to all kinds of tubes. I asked the nurse what his prognosis was, and she said his cranial pressure was quite high. It had been that way for several days. I took a minute to ask God what He wanted me to do, and He instructed me to pray.

As I was praying, the cranial pressure began to drop. I knew this was a sign from God. I asked God to allow the cranial pressure to drop down one more time as a sign of this man's recovery, and it did. Knowing this was a sign from God, I told his family he would have a full recovery, which he did.

Is it not awesome when we can pray and believe God for breakthrough on behalf of someone else, and God does it? God will never leave us without our faith being fulfilled. He wants to answer our prayers. He takes no pleasure in us praying and not receiving the fulfillment of our prayers. This miracle-working God has moved in my life, and He is still working miracles. He wants to work them for you and through you.

I have two more stories to share, and I believe they will have your faith so stirred up that you will be ready to go lay hands on the sick and watch them recover. Are you ready for God to use you to heal? No one wants to be sick, but sometimes they have been taught wrong. They have been taught that they cannot receive healing until they die, at which time they will receive their glorified body in heaven. Nothing is farther from the truth. People need their faith stirred and built up to be able to believe God for what looks impossible.

The story of how we were dispatched on a particular mission trip was quite interesting. I received a word from the Lord in which He told me there was a pastor in this nation who had seen in his dreams that an African American man would be coming to visit him. I asked a friend, who was from this nation, if he would ask around and find out who that pastor was.

He inquired about it, and sure enough, he learned about a pastor who said he had received that dream. We planned our trip, invited one of the leaders in our church to join us, and before we knew it, we were on our way. We landed in the capital city and began our five-hour journey to the city where the pastor lived. The route to arrive in the city was up a mountain via a very narrow and winding road. We drove at night, and I am glad I could not see the conditions! Right beside the road were cliffs, and parts of the road were washed away. When we finally got to the church, it was on the side of the mountain. All of the people came out to see us.

This was one of the most amazing missionary trips we have taken. The people were very hungry for the Gospel message. One lady rode a horse six hours to get there. Another lady, who was near seventy, walked for hours to get to the church. This was something I had not seen before. In our neighborhood, if it rained hard, our church members would stay at home and watch on the internet.

We arrived around nine in the evening. Some members had been at the church since nine in the morning waiting for our arrival. They were ready for a service yet that night, so we had a spontaneous church service that evening. We preached the Word and prayed. During our ministry time, my wife prayed for two members who had tumors. They were scheduled to go back to the doctor to have the tumors evaluated. We did not know it, but they were believing God for a miracle. When we returned months later, we learned that both of them had been healed miraculously of their tumors.

When God has healed you, you can believe Him for the working of healing through you for others. We had been dispatched to heal others, and God did what we were expecting Him to do.

I will share one more story to boost your faith even more. Before a church service, my wife and I were introduced to a visitor. My wife heard his story, during which she learned He had end-stage cancer and had been told that he only had a few months to live. He had come to our service for prayer.

When she shared with me that he only had a few months to live, my heart sank in my chest. I could feel his pain of living with that pronouncement of impending death. I knew what it felt like to be told there was nothing doctors could do. Even as I felt his pain, my faith swelled. The doctors might not have had a remedy, but we sure did.

I asked all our members to come closer. I made an announcement that I am sure the visitors did not understand. I asked politely that anyone who was in the service who could not believe with us for a miracle would leave the room. I know that probably is surprising, but here is why. I knew he needed a miracle, and I had not had time to fast. I only had one chance to see God perform this miracle—the time was now.

Do you remember when Jesus prayed for Jairus's daughter? Well, let me recap the story briefly (see Mark 5). Jesus was coming back from healing the demoniac of Gadarene when Jairus, who the Bible says was an official from the local synagogue, fell down at Jesus' feet. He began to beg Jesus to come heal his daughter. Jesus responded by following Jairus to his daughter. While Jesus was en route, He encountered the woman with the issue of blood, whom He healed.

By the time this was over, they received word that the ruler's daughter had died. Jesus told Jairus not to worry. The Bible shared that the people who were around them laughed because they did not believe. Jesus only allowed His three disciples and the parents of the child to be in the room. He went to her and commanded her to arise. She rose and revived.

This is where I received the revelation that no one who doubted could be in the room. I knew Jesus could heal him, and I knew he wanted to be healed. I wanted to see his healing, so we had agreement. I did not have time for disagreement to be in the room.

After I asked those who could not believe for healing to leave, we gathered around the young man and prayed. As we prayed, tears began to come to my eyes. I could feel God moving in the room. We believed God for his healing, and God did exactly what we asked Him to do. When the man went back to the doctor the next week, the doctor was amazed at the reduced amount of cancer cells he found. He asked him where he had been and what he had done. He shared that he had been to church, and the entire church had prayed for him. God sent him to us for healing, we believed God and he was healed. All we did was believe in God, believe in the Bible and it was done.

Will you accept the call from God to believe His Word for healing for someone? Will you go when God says go? God wants to dispatch you to the ends of the earth to release healing. I pray that an anointing to believe God for healing comes upon you right now. I pray that God would anoint your hands so that when people come to receive prayer, you will not be afraid of laying hands on them, and you will declare them healed. I pray that you will have the boldness and courage to be dispatched to the uttermost parts of the earth to bring glory to His name through healing. I believe that when you lay hands on others or anoint them with oil in the name of Jesus, they will receive their healing. Always remain humble and realize it is God's power operating through you.

Some people we have prayed for began to feel warmth in their hands as a signal that God is about to use them in healing. Even if that does not happen, believe God by faith, and trust Him to use you to heal. Sickness and infirmity are illegal trespassers to believers, and you are dispatched and deputized by Jesus to dispossess them of property that does not belong to them. Command sickness and infirmity to leave, command healing to come and command bodies to operate in the perfection in which God created them. God is a loving Father who wants to see all His children healed. He will send us to heal them. Now go, and believe God for healing! We are dispatched to heal!

Sent to Teach

Valora and I were invited to attend an awards dinner held in honor of exemplary educators. One of the speakers shared that the reason she taught was because she wanted to make sure her students were educated well. She knew the students she educated today could possibly be her doctor or mechanic in the future, and what she taught them gave them a better chance to be their best selves. Teachers are dispatched by God, and whether they teach in the civilian sector or the ministry, they have a vocation about which they can be passionate, because they are called to educate our future.

Thirteen books of the New Testament were written by Paul.[6] He was an amazing educator and author. While that is amazing, I am equally amazed by Paul's teacher. Whatever Gamaliel taught Paul made him willing to give up his life for what he believed in. That must have been strong, effective teaching. Moreover, everybody in most of the cities knew exactly who Paul was. He had a strong reputation for persecuting Christians. Imagine with what excellence Gamaliel must have taught Judaism to Paul. He felt the doctrine of Christians was so wrong that he was willing to haul them in chains to answer for their crimes.

This is how I want to teach disciples. I want them to love Christ so much that by the time I am done teaching them, they will live for Him no matter what. Regardless of what they are offered, they will not change. I can still remember the passion of my discipleship instructor. He taught those of us under his care a heart for discipleship. His passion and excellent instruction are the reason I am still teaching.

Recently I took my staff on a retreat. As I was sharing our vision for the next year, I shared a personal moment of reflection. I told both our campuses that I was really convicted about how we spent money in the church. I realized the budget for several departments was often two to three times more than what our children's ministry budget was. I was really saddened, and I wondered what else we could do to make it better for our children. As I shared that, our children's director began to cry. She shared that the children are left out and forgotten in many ministries. She was blessed and moved to see that God was putting the priority of our church's children on our hearts.

I am convinced teachers are vital to the future. I am committed not only to making the teaching of our children a priority, but I want to make teaching in general a priority. Only a few people say, "Pastor, I have a calling to teach." I am praying for teachers to be raised up and take their rightful places. I pray for an anointing for teachers who want to see this generation become all it was predestined to become. Let them be unmoved by the callings of others and never compare their assignment to someone else.

You will do great things. You will teach people so solidly in their beliefs that those whom you teach will become the next Paul. You will teach lawyers, doctors and nurses to be the next world changers, the next global solutionists and the next generation of think-tank geniuses. You are dispatched to teach!

Sent to Pray

When Valora grew up, her family attended a somewhat religious church. When I say religious, I mean that they were expected to have a strict adherence to a set of rules. There were rules about what you could and could not wear, about what you could or could not eat or about where you could or could not go. Most of us are familiar with the strict requirements of some Pentecostal circles of the 1970s and 1980s. You may even still be connected to them today.

She had always felt a strong calling to pray, but she had often been turned off by many of the prayers she heard. She recalls going to nights of prayer and hearing prayers such as, "Lord, if it's Your will, let me be healed." Or others such as, "Lord, You know what I need. If You would be merciful, You can answer my prayer."

She felt that this kind of prayer was begging God for what He had already given them. They did not understand that His Word was His will, and they could pray for it and see the manifestation of it through faith. For years, this was all she was exposed to. It seemed as if she heard more of people's problems being rehearsed to God than she did the power and strength of people who knew who they were in Christ. They never spoke about their covenant that allowed them to come boldly before His throne.

One day, she was invited to a women's Bible study at another church. When she arrived, a prayer meeting was being held. She was taken by surprise when she saw young, middle-aged and older ladies who were praying with power and authority. They were not what she was accustomed to, but she was drawn immediately to it.

For one, some of these women had on red nail polish and were wearing shorts. She had been told all her life that you could not pray with shorts on, and you could not wear makeup—especially not red nail polish and red lipstick. She was perplexed and caught in a conundrum. Although they were totally opposite of what she had been taught represented holiness in dress and appearance, they produced a powerful sound, and their prayers connected with God on a level she had never heard or experienced before.

She continued to sneak out to attend the ladies' fellowship with these powerful women of God. As time went on her prayer language changed. She bought every book she found on prayer, and she gave many copies to others. She made that investment willingly because she wanted to grow in her faith and prayer life, and she wanted others to come into the knowledge of freedom she was experiencing.

A book by Norvel Hayes taught her she could have what she said through confessing God's Word, and a book by Charles Capps opened her understanding of God's creative power through what we say and how we use God's Word.[7] As a result, she no longer prayed the problem; instead, she prayed the solution. She prayed the Word of God and what it said about her situation. If there was a problem, she would search for a solution in the Word of God, and then decree and declare it until it manifested.

She realized that what she had learned in her formative years was not bad, but it was incomplete. Because of those elements that were incomplete, she and others around her had been kept in bondage for years—even though they had been faithfully attending church. Most of them did not know that believers have the power to war in the Spirit for the manifestation of the promises of God. We are not sent to beg God for His promises. We are sent to intercede and pray to receive those things He has already made accessible to us in His Word and by His Spirit. These things already belong to us, but we must claim them through intercession and prayer. When you get this revelation, you will walk every day in freedom and not bondage.

Such was the case with Anna. The book of Luke mentions her as a prophetess who was sent to pray. "She was a widow of about fourscore and four years, which departed not from the temple, but served God with fastings and prayers night and day" (Luke 2:37). Some people would say this is a very boring life, but for Anna, it was the only purpose for which she was sent to earth. The Bible says she had previously been married, but only for seven years. I am not sure how old she was when she married or how old she was when the marriage ended, but the Bible does say she was now 84, and she did not leave the temple of God. She did not attempt to remarry. She gave herself totally over to the ministry of prayer and seeking God for the manifestation of His will in the earth. Oh, what would the world be like if more believers took on the ministry assignment of intercession?

I can attest that my wife, Valora, has been the catalyst to many of our prayer petitions being answered. She has a heart to pray. She recalls that as a teenager she asked God to teach her how to pray and to give her a praying spirit. He did just that. As a matter of fact, our ministry was started and founded on prayer. The first six months of our ministry consisted of nothing but prayer meetings on Friday nights.

As a result of her diligence and faithfulness in prayer, Valora has been instrumental in training intercessors all around the world. If you are feeling a tug on your heart for intercession, the Body of Christ needs you. Whether you are an intercessor who has a burden for the local church, for the marketplace, for the government or for any other area, we need you and we need your prayers. We need the strong, bold prayers that bring to pass the will of God, the plan of God and the purposes of God for His covenant people.

Our book *The Bold Prayer Warrior and Fearless Intercessor* outlines nine qualities that make up the attributes of an intercessor. You must have

- Unconditional love
- A knowledge of God's Word
- A heart of worship
- Dedication and reliability
- A teachable heart
- A heart of mercy
- Honesty and humility
- A habit of praying positive and blessing prayers
- A call and assignment to pray[8]

Every intercessor must pray with unconditional love for those for whom they are sent to pray. We must pray for everyone the same, and there can be no conditions on our love. We must have a knowledge of God's Word so that when we pray, we can pray the Word of God. We need to intercede concerning the problem, not from our emotions or feelings. We must have a heart of worship, because it is impossible to pray to a God we do not worship. As an intercessor, we must be reliable and dedicated to interceding regardless of the time of day or night upon which we are called. Intercessors are like first responders in the Spirit, and they must always be ready. People must know that when they call on us, we will pray and not stop until we receive a breakthrough.

Next, we must have a teachable heart and be moldable to the heart of God. We must have a heart of mercy. Although we may not always understand what God is doing in someone's life or situation, we must be merciful. Another attribute of an intercessor is honesty and humility. We must be people who are consistently honest with ourselves and with God. We must have a habit of always looking at and praying for the situations of others from a place of positivity and blessing. No matter what our own experiences have been or where we find ourselves in life, we must always be prepared to pray blessings upon others.

And finally, we must know that we have received a divine dispatch to pray. We cannot be willing to relent until we see the manifestation of God's perfect will in each situation on our prayer list. Some answers will come quickly, while in other situations the manifestation of our prayers may take weeks, months or even years. Think about the length of time you would want someone to pray for you. We cannot stop praying when we get tired. We must continue until we see the answer we have been believing for.

Here are a few of the verses I have committed to memory and stand on regarding prayer.

And Jesus answering saith unto them, Have faith in God. For verily I say unto you, That whosoever shall say unto this mountain, Be thou removed, and be thou cast into the sea; and shall not doubt in his heart, but shall believe that those things which he saith shall come to pass; he shall have whatsoever he saith.

Mark 11:22–23

Verily, verily, I say unto you, He that believeth on me, the works that I do shall he do also; and greater works than these shall he do; because I go unto my Father. And whatsoever ye shall ask in my name, that will I do, that the Father may be glorified in the Son. If ye shall ask any thing in my name, I will do it.

John 14:12–14

Again I say unto you, That if two of you shall agree on earth as touching any thing that they shall ask, it shall be done for them of my Father which is in heaven.

Matthew 18:19

And he spake a parable unto them to this end, that men ought always to pray, and not to faint; saying, There was in a city a judge, which feared not God, neither regarded man: and there was a widow in that city; and she came unto him, saying, Avenge me of mine adversary. And he would not for a while: but afterward he said within himself, Though I fear not God, nor regard man; yet because this widow troubleth me, I will avenge her, lest by her continual coming she weary me. And the Lord said, Hear what the unjust judge saith. And shall not God avenge his own elect, which cry day and night unto him, though he bear long with them? I tell you that he will avenge them speedily. Nevertheless when the Son of man cometh, shall he find faith on the earth?

Luke 18:1–8

Although there are many more texts you can use to pray, I have found these powerful and easy to memorize. Start with

165

these, but do not stop there. When I was in my discipleship classes, I watched a young man memorize the entire book of James. Find Scripture passages on prayer and memorize them. Do not stop until you have a memory full of verses in your arsenal of prayer. You are anointed to pray! You are called to pray!

I pray that you have a burden right now to pray. I pray you are anointed so that whatever you pray for, you see a physical manifestation of that solution. Do not get tired of praying, but have perseverance and determination. Build up your faith, and never let doubt enter your heart. I pray you are bold and courageous in your prayers, and that your petitions create a sweet-smelling aroma to God. Go forth and pray. We are dispatched to pray!

Sent to Prophesy

God used prophetic voices throughout the Bible to represent Him. Prophets were His mouthpieces to foretell, decree, establish, tear down, destroy, build and plant. We are His mouthpiece and are sent to prophesy. The Old Testament prophets point to Christ and foretell all He was going to do, while New Testament prophecy points back to Christ and all He did for us.

Jeremiah, for instance, was called and sent forth to prophesy at an early age (see Jeremiah 1). The conversation he had with the Lord is probably one that most prophetic people attempt to have with the Lord. The Word of the Lord came to Jeremiah declaring that before he was formed in the womb, God had sanctified him. He was ordained as a prophet for the nations.

Jeremiah shared his concerns with God, saying that he was only a youth and he was not able to speak. God corrected him and instructed him not to say that he was a youth. He told him that he would go wherever He sent him and that he would speak whatever the Lord told him to speak. He encouraged him by reminding him that He would be with him. He then touched Jeremiah's mouth and told him He had put His words in Jeremiah's mouth. He declared that he had set Jeremiah as a prophet to the nations.

The key word in that last sentence is *set*. Jeremiah was young. God knew that if Jeremiah was to operate as a prophet, God would have to place His words in his mouth. Because God Himself set Jeremiah as a prophet, He would have to back him up. The Hebrew word used here is the word *paqad*, which means "to appoint, assign, set over, make overseer, entrust, lay upon as a charge or commit to care."[9] Jeremiah had primary prophetic responsibility for the nations.

The Bible contains five books written by major prophetic voices. When I say *major*, I am referring to the time plan (in years) that their prophetic voice covered. These include Isaiah, Jeremiah, Ezekiel, Daniel and Lamentations (which was written by Jeremiah). Their books covered prophetic words and revelations that went far beyond the time in which they lived. In addition to the five major prophetic voices, there are twelve minor prophetic voices. Again, when I refer to minor prophetic voices, I am not saying they were any less than the major prophetic voices, but they were only sent to address a specific issue that arose in the world during their time on earth. That issue was the limit to which you heard of them.

Jonah, for instance, was sent to Nineveh. I am sure you have heard the story of Jonah, more specifically, how he was swallowed by a whale. I would like, however, to draw your attention to the bigger issue that Jonah was charged to address. When Jonah was sent to the kingdom of Nineveh, Nineveh was the capital city of the Assyrians. At the time, the children of Israel from the Northern Kingdom (composed of ten of the tribes) had been captured by Assyria. The Assyrians had not been treating the Israelites the way God desired.

By reading the whole story we learn that the Assyrians had captured the Israelites because of their disobedience. God had sent many prophets to them, but they had not listened. So, the Lord allowed the Assyrians to take them into bondage. As a result of their ill treatment of them while in captivity, the Lord sent Jonah to warn them of the impending danger and calamity the Lord would send if they did not humble themselves and repent.

Jonah knew the Lord. He knew that if the Ninevites repented, God would not destroy them. But Jonah really wanted the Lord to deal with the Assyrians harshly. So, he hesitated and did not go directly to Nineveh. He received the dispatch from the Lord, but he did not follow the instructions.

Jonah learned a lesson that would behoove many prophetic voices to learn. When God tells you to deliver a message, obey. Go and deliver the message. Because of this disobedience, Jonah spent some time in the belly of the whale. During that time in the whale, Jonah finally came to himself. How many of us have been in a metaphorical belly of the whale because of our disobedience to follow the Lord's instructions? Jonah's assignment was for that message and mission. In fact, once he delivered the message and they repented, we do not hear much of Jonah.

The next time there was a message for the Assyrians, about a hundred years from Jonah's time, the message was carried by a young prophet named Nahum. This time, unlike during Jonah's time, the people of Nineveh did not repent. As a result, God allowed the Babylonians to conquer them. Again, after Nahum's prophetic word, we do not hear much else spoken by him. This is what I mean by the length and gravity of the prophetic words spoken. Likewise, there were other prophets of Israel who never wrote books, but they had a great impact on Israel and had revelations about what Israel was doing.

I believe there are still prophets through whom God is speaking today. I believe that although you may not have a word that spans twenty or one hundred years as did some of the prophetic voices in the Bible, God still wants to speak through you. God wants to speak through you to encourage, exhort or comfort His people. I believe some were called before they were formed in their mother's wombs like Jeremiah. Others are called during adulthood, while others are used by God one time to release a serious word or revelation to the earth.

When Valora's mother became pregnant with her, she received a prophecy that Valora would be a female and would be a prophet. At a very early age, Valora remembers being a dreamer, and she remembers God speaking to her spirit. In her early years, because she did not understand how God spoke, she ignored what God was saying. As time went on and she grew in her prayer life and relationship with the Lord, she began to understand that the voice speaking to her was God's.

Maybe you do not hear the audible voice of God, but you feel His Spirit impressing things upon your heart. Or you may see in pictures, and you know the pictures are from the Lord. You may also dream, and the things you dream actually come to pass. Maybe you are like me and when the Lord speaks to you, you begin to feel a burden for something or someone you know is not your burden.

One time, I had an impression that we were being sent to a city that was not our own. For a couple of weeks before our trip, I felt heavy, almost depressed. I knew this burden was not mine—it was for someone to whom God sent me to minister. When we arrived in the city and I set foot in the church where we would minister, I knew the pastor was the person whose burden I had been carrying. Later that night after I preached the message, I asked him if I could minister to him. I began to express in words the burden I had been carrying. He acknowledged that, indeed, the burden was his. I shared that he felt alone and as if no one really had the same level of passion for ministry he carried. He felt as if he would never really reach the level of ministry God intended for him. I prayed for him, and the burden lifted off me. At the same time, he was delivered from depression and the heaviness of ministry.

God sends us to prophesy to others. He gives us a message someone desperately needs. Whether it is a message of hope, deliverance, encouragement or wisdom, it is something he or she needs to hear from the Lord.

Here are a few Scripture verses I use to hold me accountable to prophesy.

> Wherefore, brethren, covet to prophesy, and forbid not to speak with tongues.
>
> 1 Corinthians 14:39

> Follow after charity, and desire spiritual gifts, but rather that ye may prophesy. For he that speaketh in an unknown tongue speaketh not unto men, but unto God: for no man understandeth him; howbeit in the spirit he speaketh mysteries. But he that prophesieth speaketh unto men to edification, and exhortation, and comfort.
>
> 1 Corinthians 14:1–3

These are not all the verses on the prophetic and modern-day use of the prophetic ministry, of course. Along with studying these passages, I encourage you to attend a prophetic training and activation seminar so that you can learn to stir up the gift inside you. I am not saying every person is a prophet, but I do believe everyone should be able to hear from God and deliver a message from Him.

The apostle Paul encourages us to desire to prophesy. He also instructs us that our prophecy should be edifying, encouraging and comforting. This was Paul's entire reason for his second missionary trip. He went back to all the churches he had planted on the first missionary trip to encourage and strengthen them. Sometimes people need to be encouraged.

On one of the ministry trips I took out of the country, I learned the original church planter who had started the church had not had a chance to return to check on his people. It had been over ten years. The present pastor understood, but he also felt as if he had been abandoned and was all alone. The Lord gave me the word that he was not alone and that God had his back. He was sending other people to come check on him.

God may also send you to bring correction or warning. If that is the case, you must still follow through to give the word in love. I remember at a church in which I was ministering, the pastor got up and told a young man not to go out that evening. The young man listened, and his life was saved. The place he had planned to go was the scene of a mass shooting in which several people were killed, and many others were injured. If he had been there, it is likely he would have been shot.

Paul was given a prophetic warning by the prophet Agabus (see Acts 21). Agabus warned Paul he would be imprisoned if he went to Jerusalem. He took Paul's belt in his hands and said that whoever owned this belt (girdle) would be bound if he went to Jerusalem. Paul knew it was his assignment to go. Even if it cost him his life, he was still going to go. And just as Paul had to obey the assignment God had for him, Agabus had to obey the assignment to warn him. Paul did go to Jerusalem, and just as Agabus had warned, his hands and feet were bound for what he believed in.

I pray God gives you the ability to hear His voice, receive from His Spirit and deliver His Word, whether it be individually or corporately. I pray you have the ability to know when He is speaking, and that you have the boldness and courage to open your mouth and trust He will fill it with His words. I speak over you that you have the tongue of wisdom to give a word to those who are weary and need to hear instruction, wisdom and direction from God. I pray for prophetic accuracy as you yield to God.

We are dispatched to prophesy! We will encourage, exhort, edify and warn, doing all of this in love.

Sent to Bring Hope

In the early days of our ministry, I had a strong feeling we should volunteer at the women's correctional institute. Initially, Valora was challenged by the idea of going back to a prison. For her, it brought back negative memories of an experience she would have rather not encountered again.

About ten years earlier, while she was on one of her nursing assignments, she was sent to a prison. What could be difficult about going to a prison to pass out medications to inmates who had been prescribed them? Initially, it seemed harmless. As she entered, gate after gate closed behind her until she was in the secure area of the prison. She had never been so far behind so many closed gates. Thoughts began to race through her mind. What if something happened to her while she was behind the gates? What if some inmate lost his mind and attempted to attack her? How would she get out?

She arrived at the location where she was to work throughout the night until the morning. She looked through the medications she had the responsibility to pass out to the inmates and began her rounds. At first, everything was going great—until one of her greatest fears manifested. One of the inmates decided he wanted to be totally undressed as she came to his cell. He smiled with a menacing and perverted look as she brought him his medicine. She dispensed his medicine quickly, but unfortunately, the damage had been done. She could never forget what she had seen or the look in his eyes. What should have taken her a couple of hours to accomplish took her twice as many. She was truly shaken. She believed she would be scarred for life, and she told herself she would never go back into a prison again.

Fast-forward ten years, and here I was asking her to go back to a prison to mentor ladies. Every time I asked her, I noticed she was not only hesitant, but she was frightened by the idea. She finally decided to take the training and prepare to go to the prison. She and I, along with five others, went through the orientation for the prison. She received her access to the prison, and she scheduled her first day.

She was relieved to be ministering in an all-women and faith-based prison, as the administration welcomed the teaching of God's Word, and she was surprised that there were several elderly women incarcerated. As a retired nurse who specialized in geriatric nursing, her heart broke for the elderly who were in that environment. As she entered the visitation area, she marveled at the sounds of the voices she heard. One of the women was singing praises to God. Her voice sounded amazing, and it really ministered to those who listened.

Finally, they took her to a private area where she would be conducting her mentoring session. Her mentee was a young lady who had been on the waiting list for a mentor for years. After Valora introduced herself, the inmate told her she had given up hope that anyone would come mentor her. She had watched week after week as other inmates got mentorship sessions, but there had been no one for her.

As she spoke to Valora and recounted her story, her eyes began to fill with tears. She shared that in a few months she would be leaving the prison, and she was scared. She had been locked up for some time, and she had really lost touch with the reality of the things happening in the outside world. She shared that Valora coming to be a mentor was a huge blessing for her.

Her transparency and her experience hit Valora like a ton of bricks. She realized she had been selfish and disobedient in staying away from the prison and not allowing God to use her in this lady's life. Valora told her the story of how one bad prison experience almost stopped her from coming back to another prison. She shared that after that one night, she had made a promise to herself that she would never enter another prison. But something kept tugging at her heart to come and give it another chance.

Valora realized that if she had allowed the one bad experience to stop her permanently, she would never have known what it was like to bring hope to the ladies in this prison. To this day, Valora says this experience was one of the most rewarding ministry assignments she has received. She felt these women blessed her more than she could have possibly blessed them.

We cannot always choose where God will dispatch us, but we can obey. When we do, we bring immeasurable hope to someone who otherwise may not have been able to receive it. Besides this lady, Valora had an opportunity to meet, pray for and encourage many women who were in the prison. The reason they were in prison was not important. What was important was that Valora was operating in her assignment to encourage and bring hope to everyone she met in that facility.

I believe this verse is fitting: "Not forsaking the assembling of ourselves together, as the manner of some is; but exhorting one another: and so much the more, as ye see the day approaching" (Hebrews 10:25). The writer of Hebrews was writing to a church that was being persecuted. As such, there was a need to encourage them to hold fast to their profession of faith. The goal of the book of Hebrews was to encourage believers not to walk away from their faith.

> Cast not away therefore your confidence, which hath great recompence of reward. For ye have need of patience, that, after ye have done the will of God, ye might receive the promise. For yet a little while, and he that shall come will come, and will not tarry. Now the just shall live by faith: but if any man draw back, my soul shall have no pleasure in him. But we are not of them who draw back unto perdition; but of them that believe to the saving of the soul.
>
> Hebrews 10:35–39

Many believers were walking away from their faith to join other faith systems that were not as persecuted. The writer encourages them to hold on, because He who promised to come would soon be there. Does that not sound similar to today's spiritual climate? Many believers today are choosing to walk away from their faith because it is becoming difficult and unpopular to be a Christian. It is hard to uphold the principles and standards of living a life for Christ in this day and age. We will be dispatched to bring hope to the hopeless, and no matter what our experience has been in the past, we cannot allow anything to stop us. Someone's life depends on our obedience to go where He dispatches us to go.

I am reminded of a mission trip that my wife and I went on to Davao City, Philippines. We were sent by God to encourage a church and its leader. He had been preaching for years and had quite a large following, but he never had anyone sow into his life. At the end of the message, the Lord had me collect an offering for him. He said this had never been done. For twenty

years he had pastored that church, and no one had ever col-
lected an offering for him. I was amazed, because what I have
not yet shared with you was that he had become wheelchair
bound due to an accident during a spinal cord operation. Even
still, he had continued to pastor hundreds of people for several
years. He never complained because he knew he had been
sent to do the job. I am honored to call him my friend and a
brother in the Gospel.

You and I are called to bring hope and to encourage people
to hold on to their faith. I pray that if encouragement is the
area into which you are called to serve the world, God will
begin to stir your heart and strengthen your resolve to go be an
encourager of the brethren. I pray there is never a time when
you are reluctant to share the hope that is in you through
the enlightenment of God. Let your life be a source of hope.
Never be afraid to share the testimony of the work God has
done in your life. May God give you strength and boldness
to share as you have never had before. We are dispatched to
bring hope!

Sent to Fund the Work of Ministry

Finances play a key role in the work of the ministry because
of the costs associated with it. Spreading the Gospel, whether
locally or nationwide, requires money. It takes money to travel
and to provide shelter, food and clothing. It also requires
money to care for those who will receive the ministry. Local
churches need money to support the financial obligations of
rent or mortgage. They need to have a facility in which they
can assemble, empower and train, as well as have a place of
hope for the community. Money is also needed to pay for the
utilities, insurance, furniture, supplies and other obligations
of the facility.

People are needed to invest in missionaries who will take the Gospel to other nations. The Word of God commands us to feed the hungry, clothe the naked and take care of the widows and orphans. To do so, you must have continual financial support. We are commanded to give tithes and offerings to our local church to make sure these things take place and cover the expense of the house of God. When we withhold our tithes and offering, we are robbing God.

> Will a man rob God? Yet ye have robbed me. But ye say, Wherein have we robbed thee? In tithes and offerings. Ye are cursed with a curse: for ye have robbed me, even this whole nation. Bring ye all the tithes into the storehouse, that there may be meat in mine house, and prove me now herewith, saith the LORD of hosts, if I will not open you the windows of heaven, and pour you out a blessing, that there shall not be room enough to receive it. And I will rebuke the devourer for your sakes, and he shall not destroy the fruits of your ground; neither shall your vine cast her fruit before the time in the field, saith the LORD of hosts.
>
> Malachi 3:8–11

There is a blessing in honoring God with your money—the first tenth of what He has blessed you with—as well as with your offering. When we take care of God's house in supplying the money it needs to thrive, He promises to take care of our house. He will open heaven and pour out blessings in abundance. We will not just have enough for what we need, but we will have so much more than we need or can contain. He will also rebuke the devourer by preventing him from coming into our life to destroy our possessions, peace, family or anything of value connected to us.

God is looking for those He can prosper who will become generous givers. He is looking for those who are willing to bless others. He will make some people rich for the primary purpose of them being able to support the work of ministry. I believe God creates philanthropists who have created sums of wealth and whose hearts He has turned toward the funding of the Gospel.

God may make you rich enough to be generous in your giving on a regular basis. "And God is able to make all grace abound toward you; that ye, always having all sufficiency in all things, may abound to every good work" (2 Corinthians 9:8). That could mean several times a year, and not just during a specific time such as Thanksgiving or Christmas.

The book of Proverbs tells us when a man freely gives, he will gain even more, but those who withhold and keep everything for themselves and do not share with others will be brought to poverty (see Proverbs 11:24). Unfortunately, some people have the mindset that it was by their own hands they are rich. It is important to understand it was God who gave you the power to get rich. He gave you the wisdom, knowledge and understanding you needed to gain the wealth.

Whatever God does, He does it with a purpose in mind. In other words, wealth and riches are not given so that we can keep them for ourselves. Wealth is not given so that someone can brag about how much money he or she has. If wealth is given, the wealthy must not be selfish, and they must be willing to help others. God's purpose for releasing large sums of money into someone's hands is so that they can use it to advance His Kingdom. If a person is not willing to give to help others, they do not have the love of God in them. God is love because He continues to give to us every day of our lives. If we see our brother has a need, we should demonstrate the love of God and help him.

Hereby perceive we the love of God, because he laid down his life for us: and we ought to lay down our lives for the brethren. But whoso hath this world's good, and seeth his brother have need, and shutteth up his bowels of compassion from him, how dwelleth the love of God in him? My little children, let us not love in word, neither in tongue; but in deed and in truth.

1 John 3:16–18

God will raise up people He has blessed to have wealth so that they can finance the work of the Kingdom. These kinds of people fall under the ministry of helps. "And God hath set some in the church, first apostles, secondarily prophets, thirdly teachers, after that miracles, then gifts of healings, helps, governments, diversities of tongues" (1 Corinthians 12:28).

Jesus had people who were assigned to Him to support His ministry financially. Even though Jesus had an occupation, He still needed financial support. The disciples who were with Him had jobs, but they were willing to leave everything and follow Jesus; therefore, they needed support. They needed help to receive food, clothing and shelter as they traveled with Him and ministered to others. We see this support coming from those Jesus helped through healing and deliverance. We especially see this scenario in three women God used to support Jesus' ministry.

And it came to pass afterward, that he went throughout every city and village, preaching and shewing the glad tidings of the kingdom of God: and the twelve were with him, and certain women, which had been healed of evil spirits and infirmities, Mary called Magdalene, out of whom went seven devils, and Joanna the wife of Chuza Herod's steward, and Susanna, and many others, which ministered unto him of their substance.

Luke 8:1–3

179

When a church, a man or a woman of God has helped you in some way to become better equipped, you should support them financially. It is up to people like you who can ensure they have the resources needed to assist others. Even though God could have provided easily and miraculously for Jesus and His disciples, He chose to have people support them. Just as God used these amazing men and women, He wants to use you to help get the job done. He wants to use you to make sure they have enough money and resources to finish the assignment they have been dispatched to accomplish.

God is not requiring you to give to every need that arises in the Body of Christ, but it is important for you to give to your local church. This is the place where you are developed and supported in your spiritual growth. It takes discernment and wisdom to know where to place your financial obligations outside of the place you are dispatched to assist. When we understand we are only stewards over what we have—and not the real owners—we will manage our finances better. God is the sole owner; therefore, we need to ask Him what we should do with His money that He allowed us to steward. The Bible says God owns everything.

> Thine, O LORD, is the greatness, and the power, and the glory, and the victory, and the majesty: for all that is in the heaven and in the earth is thine; thine is the kingdom, O LORD, and thou art exalted as head above all. Both riches and honour come of thee, and thou reignest over all; and in thine hand is power and might; and in thine hand it is to make great, and to give strength unto all. Now therefore, our God, we thank thee, and praise thy glorious name.
>
> 1 Chronicles 29:11–13

Valora and I have seen God have many people partner with us financially as we have spread the Gospel. This has happened when we have traveled, both in the United States and several countries overseas, to put on our Suddenly meetings. When God gave us instructions and dispatched us to each location, we said yes by faith. We did not have all the money or the resources we initially needed, but we knew God would make a way for us to fulfill our assignment.

Our first conference was in Indianapolis, Indiana. God proved faithful to provide everything needed to conduct this meeting. We secured the building and purchased flights for ourselves and all our team members. We had just enough money left over from that meeting to go to the next location. Those meetings literally took us around the world, and at each place, the hand of God was manifested with signs, wonders and documented miracles of healing, restoration and breakthrough. God had specific people in place in each location to help fund our next location. Simultaneously, we actively supported other ministries who labor in the work of the Gospel.

We believe that what God orders, He pays for. You may be the next multimillionaire or billionaire God is raising up to finance the work of the Kingdom. Numerous times throughout our ministry, God touched the heart of one person in the church or in our personal ministry to fund mission trips or to purchase items we were fundraising for.

For thirteen years, we have purchased everything with cash. We have never had to purchase anything with credit, as we have always believed God to fund the work of the Kingdom. We sometimes joke that the reason our offering times take so long is because someone is writing out a million-dollar check, and they need to make sure they are spelling million correctly. My wife often says that if God must send the president on Air Force One to pay for what we need in the Kingdom, He will do it.

Know for certain God will bless you to be raised up to fund the work of the Kingdom. I pray that if this is your area of burden, God will give you witty inventions or cause you to have the kind of business in which you create large sums of wealth. I pray that God grants you discernment in knowing when to release wealth and who should receive it. I pray that He strengthens and stretches your supply of resources every time you obey Him and that He gives you an endless supply of finances to build and advance the Kingdom. We are sent to be Kingdom financiers.

Sent to Provide Solutions

I believe there are people who are born specifically for the purpose of providing solutions for the earth. I remember that when we were dispatched to Manila, Philippines, it was like the Macedonian call the apostle Paul received. One day we were live on Facebook praying for people, and a gentleman from the Philippines was online. He had been going through a particularly difficult time, and when he came across our broadcast, he said something about us jumped out to him.

He continued to watch, and each day he would see God do something amazing. As we began to travel with the message of Suddenly, he felt led to ask us to travel to his country. We had never been to the Philippines, but we had received a word from prophets in Peru that we would receive an invite to go to the Philippines. I believed that prophetic word, and I trusted that at its appointed time God would bring it to pass.

He was the dean of the College of Law at one of the state universities in the Philippines, and because of his connections, we were able to speak in front of three classes. We spoke in the morning to a class with 1,000 students, we spoke in the afternoon to a class with 1,000 students, and we spoke in the evening to a class with 600 students. The subject we spoke on was being a global solutionist. I believe God births people in the earth who are destined to provide solutions for the world's problems. Each day, students are in school to study subjects like law and science so that they can have an answer for legal and scientific situations. They are creating new laws and new scientific formulas to cure sickness and disease.

I once was given a tour of an academic cancer research program by one of the scientists. He took me to all the labs where cancer was being studied so that scientists could find a cure. I believe God is raising up people who have a burden to solve the world's problems. You may be called to solve a problem in the earth.

I remember reading the story of Moses in the desert. He found himself spending all day and night hearing the problems of the people (see Exodus 18). His father-in-law, Jethro, spoke to him and shared that if he continued to administrate in this manner, he would wear himself out. He suggested that he could save a lot of time, energy and stress by deputizing men. He thought that if he was able to put his spirit upon some of the men who were there and who had trained with him, it would keep Moses from burning out.

He chose capable men who became leaders of groups of 10, 100 or 1,000 people. This saved Moses from having to sit and listen to all the cases. This did not stop Moses from hearing the cases that needed his level of attention, but it did stop him from having to hear every single case in all Israel.

Jethro gave Moses wisdom. I believe there are Jethros who are reading this right now. I believe God has given you the ability to solve problems. Maybe it is in a field of study in which you have knowledge, or maybe it is in an area where God has gifted you naturally. Either way, you might have the strategy to solve a problem for someone else.

I was attempting to clean an area in my home, and in doing so, I had removed everything. The space looked great with nothing in it, but being able to put it all back in an organized manner is not my gift. I knew someone who was especially gifted in organization. She came over, grabbed her measuring tape and went to work organizing. She hung things from the ceiling and put items into organized bins. She even threw away some stuff I did not need anymore. When she was done, she made the area look much better.

You see, it may not be curing cancer or writing a new program, but it might be meeting a need that only God can meet through you. It might be that God has anointed and specifically gifted you to solve a problem in the earth.

If this is your burden, I pray that God would increase your ability to have keen insight into the problems the earth has. I pray that, like Jethro, you are gifted to look at problems and develop systems. God has dispatched us in the earth to find solutions for its problems.

Sent to Build, Rebuild, Rule and Reign

Moses was sent to build. He spent years erecting the tabernacle and establishing the temple system (see Exodus 25–30). After a period of time, however, the people became complacent or lacked the diligence to continue to keep the system going. As time went on, they became disobedient to God. Sometimes what we have built will be destroyed by the carnality of men; however, we can never become disobedient to what God has asked us to build and maintain.

Because of their disobedience, God allowed the enemy to come and destroy parts of King Solomon's temple. God even allowed the Northern Kingdom to be taken over by the Assyrians, and then allowed them to be taken over by the Babylonians. Unfortunately, they, too, were conquered by the Persians before they were conquered by the Greeks and

Romans. They found themselves enslaved by many different nations.

I am sure this was never God's plan. Man was led astray. As a sent one, you will be successful in whatever assignment God dispatches you on if you remain obedient and consistent in your calling. He wants you to rule and reign. He wants you to be in a position of power. He has called for you to be the one who leads.

I believe God always wants us to lead and to set the pattern for how people of faith are treated. If you fail, do not stay down. Get back up and fight with everything you have so that you remain who God says you are. None of us gets it right every time, but we must do everything within our power to lead a holy and wholesome life. We do not want to be like others who have fallen for the wrong path, and because they followed that wrong path, they no longer represent Christ's path of being divinely dispatched.

I know many leaders who started out on the path of being sent by God, but along their journey, they fell away. Now, I do not hear from them. They have lost their influence and relevance. I know several pastors and leaders who once were worldwide, but now no one ever hears of them. God wants you to rule and reign. "When the righteous are in authority, the people rejoice: but when the wicked beareth rule, the people mourn" (Proverbs 29:2).

Let's make up in our mind that, as God's delegated authority on earth, we will rule well and will always represent Him who dispatched us. He is pleased when we represent Him well. We must maintain the honor and integrity required of sent ones. There is a long-honored tradition of those who have gone before us. Let's make the declaration of the apostle Paul and say, "I have fought a good fight, I have finished my course, I have kept the faith" (2 Timothy 4:7). Let's say, as Jesus said,

"It is finished" (John 19:30). This is the salutation that every sent one desires to place on his or her tombstone. Jesus was a sent one, and He finished well the course laid out before Him. You are a sent one. You are dispatched to build, rebuild, rule and reign.

Enemies of Your Divine Dispatch

Let's take a minute to assess and identify enemies to your assignment. Although I wish it was not so, you will experience challenges and tribulations; however, be encouraged by the words of Paul the apostle. "For our light affliction, which is but for a moment, worketh for us a far more exceeding and eternal weight of glory" (2 Corinthians 4:17).

There are two types of opposition: opposition that comes from the inside, and opposition that comes from the outside. Both can be damaging to your assignment if not brought under control.

Internal opposition is often self-inflicted. We have areas in which we have caused ourselves harm. Some things that have sidetracked sent ones include

- Greed and lust for money
- Pride and overinflated or overestimated self-image
- Perversion of gifts for self-gain

- Competition or comparison with others
- Vanity
- Anti-submissiveness
- Unteachable spirit
- Cynicism
- Callousness
- Rejection
- Abandonment
- Fear of failing again based on failures of the past
- Fear of man
- Desire to prove our own worth
- Compromise

We must get control of these, because we can control them. We do not have to allow them to control us. We must master ourselves and be like Paul the apostle when he said, "But I keep under my body, and bring it into subjection: lest that by any means, when I have preached to others, I myself should be a castaway" (1 Corinthians 9:27). Another translation says, "But [like a boxer] I buffet my body [handle it roughly]" (AMPC). We must be like him in this and discipline our flesh, mind, will and emotions to be trained and focused. We will not allow the enemy to prevail.

Not all of the opposition we will experience comes from inside. Some of the warfare will come from external factors. But do not worry, God has them under control.

Some of the external opposition that we will encounter includes

- Spirits of religion in regions and territories
- Familial spirits

- Seducing spirits
- Jezebel spirits
- Absalom spirits
- Bewitchers

It is always challenging when you enter a region in which there is a controlling spirit. Many times, religions or people who are the controlling figures in the regions will present a problem. When Nehemiah, for instance, went back to Jerusalem, the people who fought him the hardest were Tobiah and Sanballat (see Nehemiah 4). They had been in control in the region and did not want the Israelites to rebuild the temple. They even wrote letters to the rulers to get them to stop. But Nehemiah persevered and completed the wall.

Moses encountered family spirits like Korah, who was a cousin, and Miriam, who was a sister. They suffered for opposing Moses (see Numbers 12, 16). People may harass you, but they do not have the power to stop you. Keep going and prevail in Jesus' name.

In another story, Jezebel brought some stress to Elijah, but she could not prevail either (see 1 Kings 18–19). She eventually received her just recompense for trying to stop the work of the Kingdom. Absalom was a son of King David who was upset with his father and tried to lead a rebellion (see 2 Samuel 15). In the end, he failed. The apostle Paul dealt with what I call bewitchers (see Galatians 3). After he had preached in a city, he found people went back and whispered in the ears of his disciples to get them to leave Paul's teaching—and some listened.

Although sent ones hate to encounter these spirits, the truth is that they will always be there in one form or another. We will always have to deal with them; however, the good news is that they were not successful against David, Paul, Elijah or Moses, and they will not prevail and succeed with us. I am glad the Word of God is on our side. It declares, "No weapon that is formed against thee shall prosper" (Isaiah 54:17).

Declarations, Decrees, Confessions and Prayers

We believe in the power of confession and prayer. In fact, our ministry was birthed out of these elements. The world we live in is shaped by the words we speak consistently and continually. It is important for every believer to have a disciplined habit of both prayer and positive confession. No matter what your circumstances look like or what is going on around you, the key is to remain steadfast in your confessions and to believe God for them to manifest.

Sent One Creed

I am a Sent One. I was not just born, but I was divinely dispatched into the earth by the King of kings and the Lord of lords who is the Great I Am to solve a problem and provide an answer on the earth.

I am a Sent One. I am a problem solver, I am a history maker and I am a change agent. I am creative, and I have all the wisdom and power of the Spirit of God working and operating in and through me to complete every assignment I have been given.

I am a Sent One. I have been given every weapon, resource and skill necessary to complete the mission I have been given.

I am a Sent One. My message is that of the Kingdom of God. I have a mantle, mission and mandate. My burden is that of my Lord and Savior, Jesus Christ, which is the burden for souls to be saved and disciples to be made.

I am a Sent One. I will not retreat, surrender or throw in the towel until I have completed my assignment and have heard the words, "Well done, good and faithful servant," from my Commander-in-Chief!

I am a Sent One.

Declarations and Decrees

- I was created and dispatched into the earth by God to fulfill His assignment for my life.
- God's plan for my life is very good because of its purpose (see Genesis 1).
- I am royalty, I am holy and I have been chosen by God to do great things in the earth (see 1 Peter 2:9).
- I daily present my body unto God as a living sacrifice, holy and acceptable (see Romans 12:1).
- I am a slave and a prisoner of Christ, I walk worthy of my calling and I willingly serve Him every day of my life (see Ephesians 4:1–16).
- I surrender my will, mind and emotions in exchange for God's will, His mind and His emotions (see Matthew 10:39).
- God has given me all things that pertain to life and godliness (see 2 Peter 1:3).
- God has given me a Kingdom vision of how I fit in His divine plan (see Ephesians 3:16–17).
- I have a prophetic voice to govern and rule over kingdoms and nations (see Jeremiah 1:9–10).
- I will be steadfast, unmovable and always abounding in the work of God, knowing that my labor is not in vain (see 1 Corinthians 15:58).
- No weapon formed against me will prosper, and I condemn words spoken against me (see Isaiah 54:17).
- I will not allow anything or anyone to separate me from my relationship with God (see Romans 8:31–39).

- Because the Lord is my helper, I will not be afraid of man and what he can do to me, knowing I will look in triumph on my enemies (see Psalm 118:6–7).
- God has given His angels charge over me to keep and protect me (see Psalm 91).
- I am confident in knowing that what God started in me will be completed (see Philippians 1:6).
- I take authority over every principality and ruler of darkness in territories and regions, and I cast down everything that attempts to rise above God's knowledge in my life (see 2 Corinthians 10:5–7).
- I am more than a conqueror through Christ Jesus (see Romans 8:37).
- When I go into an area and people do not receive me or hear the word given to me, I will shake the dust from my feet and keep going (see Matthew 10:14).
- I will work as unto God, and I will seek His approval and not the acceptance of man (see Colossians 3:23).
- I follow Jesus. Because I have the mind of Christ, I act like Him. Just as Christ is, so am I (see 1 Corinthians 2:16).
- I will not walk in condemnation, because I am a new creation in Christ. Old sins, habits and shortcomings have passed away, and now I am walking in the new (see Romans 8:1).
- I will be fearless in the face of adversity (see Psalm 23:4).
- I will not be moved out of purpose or neglect my assignment (see 1 Timothy 4:14).

Confessions

- I have been dispatched by God to bring healing, restoration and deliverance to others (see Mark 16:15–18).
- The divine resources of finances and personnel I need to complete my assignment have been released in the earth (see Philippians 4:19).
- I will meet the right person at the right time to open the right doors (see Ruth 2:11–12).
- Divine favor is my portion to open every door that needs to be opened (see Luke 2:52).
- Favor in the Church, business, government and marketplace is facilitating my divine assignment (see Psalm 5:12).
- Kings are assigned to support my Kingdom assignment (see Nehemiah 2:4–8).
- Laws are being changed to cooperate with my assignment (see Esther 8:7–12).
- I have been given every weapon necessary to fight and win in my area of dispatchment (see 2 Corinthians 10:4–6).
- Angels have been assigned to me for the completion of my assignment (see Psalm 91:11–12).
- Divine alignments, assignments and connections in heaven and earth are in my favor (see Romans 8:28).
- I have the ox anointing operating in my life to accomplish great tasks (see Proverbs 14:4).[1]

Prayer of a Sent One

FATHER GOD, *You are my Creator, and I am amazed at Your handiwork. You knew me before I was in my mother's womb, and You decided what I would look like and what I would do in life. You knit me together, and I praise You because I am fearfully and wonderfully made in Your image.*

You called me according to Your purpose and dispatched me into the earth as Your ambassador. You have given me power over nations and the authority to speak on Your behalf to advance the Kingdom. Even though this assignment is substantial, I know You have equipped me with what I need to fulfill it. I cannot and will not try to do it by my own understanding, power or might, but will only rely on Your Spirit, who lives inside of me. Holy Spirit, I trust in You to be my Comforter and my Guide who walks beside me, to lead me to the truth and to be the power I need to overcome all the other opposing forces in the earth. In those times when I do not feel qualified to do it, help me to trust in You and not depend on what I know. Stir up the gifts inside of me for me to fully operate in with boldness and confidence. I seek divine wisdom to know what to do with what You have given to me. Thank You for freely giving it to me.

In addition to wisdom, I desire understanding and clarity of my assignment. I call forth the release of words of knowledge to be activated in my life as I minister and bring insight to others. I desire the gift of healing to be stirred in me to see others healed of all manner of sickness and disease. As You release it, I receive the gift of prophecy that I may bring edification, exhortation and comfort to others. I desire the gift of discernment that I may know who is of You and who has been sent by the enemy. I want to discern the times and the seasons of what You are doing in my life so that I do not miss any opportunities.

Father God, teach me Your laws and Your statutes, and I will obey them with my whole heart. Open the eyes of my understanding to Your Word. I will put Your Word in my heart so that I will not sin against You. As a leader, help me to remain humble and prevent pride from operating in me during my assignment. I pray the fruit of the Spirit will be evident through my life in everything I do. I surrender completely to Your perfect will in exchange for mine, knowing Your will has always brought me the best results.

Show me the people You have assigned to me in this season and give me the courage to release those You are removing or have not assigned to me. I welcome intercessors and prophets who will cover and guard me diligently. Protect me from the evil one, who desires to destroy me and stop me from fulfilling my destiny. Help me to be vigilant and aware of his plots, plans and schemes so that I may not fall into temptation. I cover myself with the blood of Jesus and release Your Word to prevent any attack on my life. Let Your will be done in my life even as it is in heaven. In Jesus' name, Amen.

Conclusion

*O*ur prayer is that you have understood fully that you were sent into the earth for much more than just living. We pray that reading this book has given you the ability to see life through the lens of a sent one. You were born to fulfill a role. That role is so significant that no one else can do it. God has sent and divinely dispatched you into the earth to solve problems and present the character, mind and heart of Christ to the people He loves. Jesus knew He would be returning to heaven and would need representatives to continue the work long after He left. He promised never to leave us or forsake us.

I am honored that God chose my wife and me to write this book and to share what we believe is His heart for us. I pray that as you journey on your path of dispatch, no matter where it takes you, you will always honor the Lord who sent you as well as those other brothers and sisters who have represented Him in the earth. Being a sent one is a time-honored tradition and calling that goes much deeper than we realize.

I pray you will have the strength to always do the right thing when the tough situations arise. May you always remember the day you met Him and the day you said yes to Him. He is committed to you, and He expects you to be committed to your call and to your yes to Him.

God bless and keep you as you journey on your divine dispatch!

LaJun and Valora

Notes

Introduction

1. In this book, I will use the terms *sent one* to speak of the person whom God sends and *divine dispatch* to refer to the assignment. At times, the two terms may be used interchangeably.

2. *Merriam-Webster*, s.v. "divine," accessed March 23, 2022, https://www.merriam-webster.com/dictionary/divine.

3. *Merriam-Webster*, s.v. "dispatch," accessed March 23, 2022, https://www.merriam-webster.com/dictionary/dispatch.

4. Blue Letter Bible, s.v. "apostello" (Strong's G649), accessed March 23, 2022, https://www.blueletterbible.org/lexicon/g649/kjv/tr/0-1/.

5. Bible Hub, s.v. "575.apo," accessed March 23, 2022, https://biblehub.com/greek/575.htm.

6. Bible Tools, s.v. "stello" (Strong's 4724), accessed March 23, 2022, https://www.bibletools.org/index.cfm/fuseaction/Lexicon.show/ID/G4724/stello.htm.

7. Bible Study Tools, s.v. "pempo" (Strong's 3992), accessed March 23, 2022, https://www.biblestudytools.com/lexicons/greek/kjv/pempo.html.

8. Blue Letter Bible, s.v. "matheteuo" (Strong's G3100), accessed March 23, 2022, https://www.blueletterbible.org/lexicon/g3100/kjv/tr/0-1/.

9. Bible Tools, s.v. "baptizo" (Strong's 907), accessed March 23, 2022, https://www.bibletools.org/index.cfm/fuseaction/Lexicon.show/ID/G907/baptizo.htm.

10. Blue Letter Bible, s.v. "kerysso" (Strong's G2784), accessed March 23, 2022, https://www.blueletterbible.org/lexicon/g2784/kjv/tr/0-1/.

11. Bible Study Tools, s.v. "exousia" (Strong's 1849), accessed March 23, 2022 https://www.biblestudytools.com/lexicons/greek/kjv/exousia.html.

Stage 1 Discovery

1. Dictionary.com, s.v. "discover," accessed March 23, 2022, https://www.dictionary.com/browse/discover.

Chapter 1 Discovery in Dreams

1. *Merriam-Webster*, s.v. "obeisance," accessed March 23, 2022, https://www.merriam-webster.com/dictionary/obeisance.
2. Blue Letter Bible, s.v. "samar" (Strong's H8104), accessed March 23, 2022, https://www.blueletterbible.org/lexicon/h8104/kjv/wlc/0-1/.

Chapter 3 Discovery by Prophecy

1. *An Officer and a Gentleman*, directed by Taylor Hackford (Hollywood, CA: Paramount Pictures, 1982).

Chapter 6 Development in the Life of Paul

1. Bible Study Tools, s.v. "kabowd" (Strong's 03519), accessed March 23, 2022, https://www.biblestudytools.com/lexicons/hebrew/kjv/kabowd.html.

Chapter 10 Development in the Life of Peter

1. Blue Letter Bible, s.v. "pistis" (Strong's G4102), accessed March 23, 2022, https://www.blueletterbible.org/lexicon/g4102/kjv/tr/0-1/.
2. Blue Letter Bible, s.v. "areté" (Strong's 703), accessed March 23, 2022, https://www.blueletterbible.org/lexicon/g703/kjv/tr/0-1/.
3. Blue Letter Bible, s.v. "gnosis" (Strong's G1108), accessed March 23, 2022, https://www.blueletterbible.org/lexicon/g1108/kjv/tr/0-1/.
4. Blue Letter Bible, s.v. "egkrateia" (Strong's G1466), accessed March 23, 2022, https://www.blueletterbible.org/lexicon/g1466/kjv/tr/0-1/.
5. Dictionary.com, s.v. "master," accessed March 23, 2022, https://www.dictionary.com/browse/master.
6. Blue Letter Bible, s.v. "hypomonē" (Strong's G5281), accessed March 23, 2022, https://www.blueletterbible.org/lexicon/g1466/kjv/tr/0-1/.
7. Blue Letter Bible, s.v. "eusebeia" (Strong's G2150), accessed March 23, 2022, https://www.blueletterbible.org/lexicon/g2150/kjv/tr/0-1/.
8. Blue Letter Bible, s.v. "agape" (Strong's G26), accessed March 23, 2022, https://www.blueletterbible.org/lexicon/g26/kjv/tr/0-1/.

Stage 3 Deployment

1. Oxford Learner's Dictionaries, s.v. "deployment," accessed March 23, 2022, https://www.oxfordlearnersdictionaries.com/us/definition/english/deployment?q=deployment.

Chapter 11 Who Is Sent?

1. Blue Letter Bible, s.v. "shalach" (Strong's H7971), accessed March 23, 2022, https://www.blueletterbible.org/lexicon/h7971/kjv/wlc/0-1/.
2. Blue Letter Bible, s.v. "shilluwach" (Strong's H7971), accessed March 23, 2022, https://www.blueletterbible.org/lexicon/h7964/vul/wlc/0-1/.

Chapter 12 How Are We Sent?

1. Blue Letter Bible, s.v. "dynamis" (Strong's G1411), accessed March 23, 2022, https://www.blueletterbible.org/lexicon/g1411/kjv/tr/0-1/.
2. Blue Letter Bible, s.v. "exousia" (Strong's G1849), accessed March 23, 2022, https://www.blueletterbible.org/lexicon/g1849/kjv/tr/0-1/.
3. Blue Letter Bible, "The Names of God in the Old Testament," accessed March 23, 2022, https://www.blueletterbible.org/study/misc/name_god.cfm.

Chapter 13 What Are We Sent to Do?

1. *Merriam-Webster*, s.v. "syncretism," accessed March 23, 2022, https://www.merriam-webster.com/dictionary/syncretism.
2. Bible Study Tools, s.v. "legion," accessed March 23, 2022, https://www.biblestudytools.com/dictionary/legion/.
3. The Fearless Challenge is an online challenge that is organized by Valora as part of her Fearless Women Global Organization (www.fearlesswomenglobal.org). Women who have overcome tremendous encounters with fear have the opportunity to share their testimonies.
4. SWAT is an acronym that stands for Special Weapons and Tactics, and they are groups of highly trained American policemen who deal with the most dangerous criminals.
5. I had been reading *Smith Wigglesworth on Spiritual Gifts, Smith Wigglesworth on Healing, Smith Wigglesworth on the Anointing, Smith Wigglesworth on the Holy Spirit,* and *Ever Increasing Faith.*
6. Pamela Palmer, "How Many Books of the Bible Did Paul Write," Bible Study Tools, September 8, 2021, https://www.biblestudytools.com/bible-study/topical-studies/how-many-books-of-the-bible-did-paul-write.html.
7. Those books were *You Can Have What You Say* by Norvel Hayes and *God's Creative Power* by Charles Capps.
8. LaJun M. Cole Sr. and Valora Shaw-Cole, *The Bold Prayer Warrior and Fearless Intercessor: Prayers That Bring Breakthrough* (Tampa, Fla.: LaJun and Valora Cole Ministries, 2017).
9. Blue Letter Bible, s.v. "paqad" (Strong's H6485), accessed March 23, 2022, https://www.blueletterbible.org/lexicon/h6485/kjv/wlc/0-1/.

Declarations, Decrees, Prayers and Confessions

1. It is my opinion that the ox anointing is indicative of the sent one. Sent ones are steady, they work long years, they have great strength and they produce great increase for the Kingdom of God.

LaJun and Valora Cole are a ministry power team based in Tampa, Florida, who have a mission to empower, equip and encourage believers worldwide. They are respected both nationally and internationally as pastors, authors, entrepreneurs and leaders who use their voices to share God's hope to the Body of Christ.

LaJun and Valora are contributing columnists to *Charisma* magazine, as well as podcast hosts of *Prophetic Moments with LaJun & Valora* on Charisma Podcast Network. They have published over twenty books. They serve as the founding and global lead pastors of Contagious Church, which is a multi-site church with campuses in Tampa, Florida, and Charlotte, North Carolina. The church has a mission to make the love, faith and worship of Christ contagious.

They also lead Contagious Connexion, which is a global network of churches, ministries, pastors and entrepreneurs who are connected in covenant to collaborate, build and advance the Kingdom of God. They founded the Discipleship Training Institute in 2010 with the mission of helping believers discover, develop and deploy their gifts and assignments.

In addition to their not-for-profit endeavors, they also lead several for-profit entities. Exponential Group Global has a mission to assist visionaries as they maximize their potential and increase and enhance their capacity. They are founders of Cole and Company Global, with its newest venture, Cole

Seasonings, which has as its mission to produce healthy and hearty premium seasonings.

Valora serves as president of the board of directors for Bay Area Charter and the Florida Education Charter Foundation, where she oversees fifteen charter schools throughout the state of Florida. She is the founding president of Fearless Women Global, which is an organization of women with a mission to inspire, encourage and connect. She also serves as the president and CEO of Contagious Cares, which has a mission to produce sustainable change in global communities through education and economic development.

LaJun is a thirteen-year United States Army veteran whose job titles include drill sergeant, sapper and platoon sergeant. Valora is a retired pediatric and geriatric nurse. They are the proud parents of three sons, one daughter, eight grandchildren and a host of spiritual sons and daughters around the globe.

Together, under the banner of LaJun and Valora Cole Ministries, they have traveled to over 100 cities within the United States and 29 foreign nations. They have also appeared on CTN, TBN and other major Christian television and radio programs around the globe helping believers discover, develop and deploy their God-given purpose, power and potential.

For more information about LaJun and Valora, please visit their website at www.lajunandvalora.com. You may email them at info@lajunandvalora.com, or you may call them at 1844WeRCOLE (1-844-937-2653). You can also follow them on Facebook, Instagram, YouTube, TikTok, Twitter and Clubhouse under their joint name, LaJun and Valora. You can download their app on Google and iTunes under Contagious Church or LaJun and Valora Cole Ministries.